God Loves My Kitchen Best

God Loves My Kitchen Best

MAB GRAFF

ZONDERVAN
PUBLISHING HOUSE
OF THE ZONDERVAN CORPORATION | GRAND RAPIDS, MICHIGAN 49506

Scripture quotations, unless otherwise indicated, are from *The Revised Standard Version* in the Old Testament and *The New International Version —New Testament* in the New Testament. *The Revised Standard Version* is copyright © 1946, 1952 by the Division of Christian Education of the National Council of Churches of Christ in the United States of America. *The New International Version* is copyright © 1973 by the New York International Bible Society. The *King James Version* is also used where indicated.

God Loves My Kitchen Best
© 1977 by The Zondervan Corporation
Grand Rapids, Michigan

Library of Congress Cataloging in Publication Data

Graff, Mab.
    God loves my kitchen best.

    1.   Wives — Prayer-books and devotions — English.
I. Title.
BV4844.G7   242'.6'43   77-5618

ISBN 0-310-35612-1

Printed in the United States of America.

83   84   85   86   87   88 — 20   19   18

CONTENTS

God Loves My
Kitchen Best

HOUR OF SHOWER

THE BACK OF THE CHURCH BULLETIN WAS blank. I wrote on it, "Shirley is five months pregnant. Let's give her a shower." I gave the note to my friend Dorothy, who sits next to me in the choir loft. Then I folded my hands angelically and looked at the pastor's back while he made some announcements. Dorothy nudged me and handed back the bulletin. She had written, "Okay by me. My house or yours — or fellowship hall?"

We passed the bulletin back and forth until every blank space was covered. During the offertory we started on her bulletin, and by the time the service was over, we had scribbled all over it, too.

"How was church?" my husband asked as I put my purse and Bible on the coffee table.

"Fine," I said. "Too bad you had to work." I sat down and kicked off my shoes. "Dorothy and I are going to give Shirley a baby shower." He nodded agreement.

"Where?"

"At church, I think," I said, "if I can clear a date. We've

got it all planned. I'll send out the invitations, and Dorothy will take care of the games. We'll each bake two cakes, and I'll buy the ice cream and nuts. She'll buy the prizes and decorations." I took a deep breath. "We'll keep account and split the costs."

"You have got it all figured out," he said. "So — how was the sermon?"

"Uh — great."

"What did he preach on?"

"Uh — let me get dinner started and then I'll tell you." I went into the kitchen and leaned against the counter. I couldn't think of one word of the sermon!

"What did the choir sing?" he called. Good grief! I couldn't even remember what we sang!

"Just a minute, honey, and I'll come back and talk to you." How could I admit I had been so absorbed in plans for the shower I had blocked out the entire worship hour? Maybe if I stayed in the kitchen long enough he'd forget about it. I began to hum loudly, open and shut the refrigerator door, bang lids, and rattle silverware. He didn't ask any more questions. In fact, he was so quiet I thought he'd gone outside. I peeked into the living room, and he was reading the church bulletin. Looking up, he grinned at me.

"No wonder you don't know what the preacher said."

"Well," I said defensively, "Dorothy's going to be gone all this week. We had to get it planned!" He raised his eyebrows, and I flounced into the kitchen.

Which reminds me — we didn't decide whether to use church dishes or buy paper plates. No matter. We can decide that next Sunday during church.

10

"The Lord said: '... this people draw near with their mouth and honor me with their lips, while their hearts are far from me ...'" (Isa. 29:13).

Because we are saved by God's grace and not by our works, we often tend to be too casual when we worship our wonderful, holy Lord.

FALSE EYELASHES

MY HUSBAND'S COMPANY HAD SCHEDULED A big party and I wanted to look my best, so I decided to buy a pair of false eyelashes. I had a hard time deciding which kind to buy. Should I choose the heavy, black ones that looked like caterpillars, or the sparse, brown ones that looked like centipedes? I finally settled for an innocent-looking brown pair, sound asleep in their plastic box.

The afternoon of the party I began to get ready early, and it's a good thing, because it took me an hour to get the eyelashes on. The directions said to first measure your eyes and then cut the lashes to fit. Well, I poked the corner of the ruler in my right eye, and it wouldn't quit watering for about fifteen minutes. I should have used a tape measure, but I couldn't find it. I think I threw it out the time I found out my measurements were 32-30-42. Anyway, after I got the eyelashes trimmed to fit, the directions said to flex them back and forth so they would conform to the eyelid. I flexed one of them right into the bathtub.

The next step was to spread a thin row of adhesive along the edge and let it dry for one minute. When I started to pick up the eyelash, it had rolled over and was stuck on the tile. I got it lose, but it was bent in the shape of an *L*.

The instructions said the best way to apply them was to lay a mirror on a flat surface and look into it with your eyes half closed, grasp the lash in the center, and place it next to your own lashes. This was hard for me, because without my glasses I can't even see my *own* eyelashes. First I stuck the lash in my eye, and does that glue burn! I kept trying, either getting it too high, or out on my own lashes. I decided maybe I ought to try the left lash, and amazingly I got it on and in the right place the first try. I was stunned at how beautiful my left eye looked. My right eye, however, looked like a bad case of conjunctivitis, and there were little balls of glue all over the eyelid.

At last I did get the other lashes on, so I stood back and batted my eyelashes at myself. Wow! I almost looked glamorous.

In my new long dress, loop earrings, and false eyelashes, I sauntered up to my husband and fluttered my eyelids at him.

"Notice anything different?" I said huskily.

"You got a cold?" he asked. "You're eyes are blood-shot."

The directions said, "To remove, grasp at outer edge and peel off gently." I ripped them off and flushed them down the toilet. And then I opened the medicine cabinet and took out a package of Contac. Maybe I did have a cold — both my eyes were running.

" . . . you enlarge your eyes with paint? In vain you beautify yourself . . ." (Jer. 4:30).

"Instead, it should be that of your inner self, the un-fading beauty of a gentle and quiet spirit, which is of great worth in God's sight" (1 Peter 3:4).

We should do the best we can with our natural attributes, but we'll be even prettier if we concentrate on the beauty of a gentle spirit.

SUPER STRENGTH

I WOKE UP THIS MORNING SICK TO MY stomach and with a terrible headache. It hurt to swallow, and my temperature was 101 degrees. I was so dizzy I could barely stand while I fixed breakfast and made lunches. And this was the day a friend and I were going shopping at the new center and then out to lunch.

As soon as everyone left, I called my friend.

"Dorothy," I croaked, "I'm sorry but I'm sick. I can't go."

"Oh, no! We were going to have such fun today."

"I know. But I'm going right back to bed."

"Poor kid. I'll be over in about an hour."

"Why?"

"I'm going to do your work this morning."

What a sweet friend, I thought, as I stood up shakily and stumbled over a stack of books on the floor. I looked around at the living room. It looked like a rummage sale. There was a parcheesi game and crayons on the coffee table, a few peanut shells on the carpet, several socks draped here and there, a Mickey Mouse T-shirt on the floor, and an empty donut box behind the TV.

Through Dorothy's eyes, I looked at the catastrophe in

the kitchen. Spilled cereal crunched underfoot. My bedroom slipper stuck slightly in the place where one of the kids had spilled pop. The dishwasher was full of clean dishes, and the sink and table were full of dirty ones. I thought I might throw up, so I hurried to the bathroom.

There were several towels on the floor, some green blobs of toothpaste in the lavatory, and a long dribble of something red — I hoped it wasn't blood — on one of the cupboard doors. As I crept back to bed, my misery was increased by the thought of my friend seeing this house at its nauseating worst. I lay there a few moments, trying to compose a reasonable excuse.

Suddenly I found the strength to leap out of bed. Like the White Tornado I roared through the house, grabbing up clothes, straightening, putting away, scrubbing, vacuuming, dusting. I even changed the sheets and took a shower before Dorothy came. By the time she arrived, there was nothing left for her to do.

"I don't see how you keep your house so straight," she said, bewildered.

I shrugged, too weak and sick to comment.

I still feel terrible and my temperature is 102 degrees. But my house is cleaner than it's been for weeks.

" . . . the LORD; He is their strength in the time of trouble" (Ps. 37:39 KJV).

"And the God of all grace, who called you to his eternal glory in Christ, after you have suffered a little while, will himself restore you and make you strong, firm, and steadfast" (1 Peter 5:10).

The Lord can give us super strength — but sometimes He allows us to suffer to strengthen us spiritually.

16

HAWAIIAN CHICKEN

ONE EVENING, IN AN INSANE MOMENT OF cordiality, I invited five couples for dinner from my husband's place of employment. The next day I almost fainted when I realized that ten people would be looking to me to feed them. Terror grabbed me in the stomach when I thought of our small house, the chipped china, and the worn carpet. Worst of all was the fact that I am an exceptionally bad cook. What had gotten into me to let myself in for such torture? What could I serve? I thought of my two stand-bys: spaghetti and meatballs or goulash. Unthinkable. I began to cry.

"How about a nice roast?" my mother suggested on the phone.

"You know I can't cook roast," I wailed. "That's how you cracked your bridge, remember? Besides, trying to cut the meat and get the potatoes mashed and everything on before it gets cold —" I began to tremble. "I've got to hang up, mother. I feel sick."

If only I *could* get sick and go to the hospital. I could see myself huddled on a bed of pain, near death and free from worry. Dear Father, is there a solution?

"Why not give a luau?" a good friend suggested.

"I can't even spell it," I moaned. "Anyway, I'd ruin it."

"No you won't. I have this simple and delicious recipe, 'Hawaiian Chicken,' and you could serve it right out of the pan. You can have fresh fruits and salads, and serve it buffet-style. Invite your guests to wear muumuus and bright shirts, and play Hawaiian music. You'll have fun!"

Preparing the dinner was fairly simple. I put twelve pounds of chicken pieces, covered with onions, molasses, celery, mushrooms, brown sugar, pineapple, peppers, and soy sauce, in the oven before noon, and then I fixed all kinds of raw "finger foods." By seven o'clock everything was ready; I had a flower in my hair; and people were coming up the walk yelling, "Aloha!"

At dinner I noticed the buffet line wasn't moving.

"Can't decide which piece?" I heard a guest say.

"I don't care which piece. I just can't get it out."

"Here, give me the fork," one man said. It was no use. All twelve pounds were stuck fast in a carmelized grip. Suddenly he flipped a bone out across the room. My husband closed his eyes.

Rallying, I said, "Honey, could you carve?"

"Carve?" he muttered. "We need a chisel."

He finally got a knife under it, and it wasn't long until everyone had a piece. It wasn't too bad — kind of like eating peanut brittle.

The evening had been a lot of fun, I decided the next day while I was cleaning up the mess. Some of the guests had harmonized on Hawaiian songs while others tried to hula. I got better acquainted with some of the people, and others seemed content to just sit and suck on their chicken bones. I think the evening was a success.

"While Jesus was having dinner at Levi's house, many tax collectors and 'sinners' were eating with him . . ." (Mark 2:15).

If we open our homes to those without Christ, some may open their hearts to Him.

COFFEE FREAK

I'VE GOTTEN INTO THE HABIT OF TAKING a cup of coffee with me in the car, because I'm usually late and haven't finished my meal when it's time to leave home. Anyway, I've got this neat little cup that fits in a certain groove on the instrument panel, and I get a lot of pleasure out of driving along, sipping my coffee.

One morning on the way to mother's, I was rolling along the freeway, trying to change lanes without hitting any of the buttons, when that little cup of hot coffee came ungrooved, slid across the panel, and dumped in my lap. There's not a lot you can do except keep driving when you're in the center lane of the freeway, even if your stomach and legs are scalded. I'm sure I must have yelled because the man on my left looked startled and shot ahead like a dragster.

After the coffee cooled down, I realized what a mess I was in. Six ounces is a lot of wet when you don't have anything to mop with but a used tissue. The worst part was that I had promised mother I would stop at the drugstore and pick up her prescription.

I carried my purse so it covered most of the brown stain

on my pants, but while waiting at the prescription desk the lady next to me said, "Mmm! Doesn't that coffee smell good! They must have added a coffee shop."

I paid for the medicine, hurried over to the perfume counter, and grabbed a sample dispenser bottle at random. I aimed it at my chest, gave it a hard jab, and a big blob of hand lotion slithered down my blouse.

When I finally arrived at mother's house, she greeted me with a big hug and then sniffed.

"Honey, you smell like coffee."

I explained it to her while I sponged off the coffee and hand lotion stains.

"Well, I hope you've learned your lesson," she admonished. "You could have had a serious accident."

When it was time to go, she looked at the table and asked, "Is there anything here you'd like to take with you?"

"I'll run get my cup," I said. "I think there's a little coffee left."

"The way of a fool is right in his own eyes, but a wise man listens to advice" (Prov. 12:15).

"And you have forgotten the word of encouragement . . . do not make light the Lord's discipline, and do not lose heart when he rebukes you" (Heb. 12:5).

It's hard to change our ways or admit we were wrong, but it's easier than to endure the Lord's punishment.

INSUFFICIENT FUNDS

WHEN MY HUSBAND CAME IN THIS EVE-
ning with his lower lip stuck out I knew I'd done something
wrong. He held out a check, and the words *Insufficient
Funds* jumped out at me.

"Oh, no, not again!"

"The check I wrote for the company excursion
bounced! And the gal brought it back to me, in front of the
boss!"

"Well it's not my fault," I said, too scared to look him in
the eye. "Is it?"

"Of course it's your fault. Your balance showed two
hundred dollars!"

What on earth could have happened? Sure, I always
have trouble subtracting, but two hundred dollars' worth?
Besides, it seemed to me I had plenty of money this pay
period. I had even bought some shoes and extra things for
the house.

"I'm sure there's just been a mistake," I said.

"The mistake was when I gave you back the
checkbook." I knew then he was going to take away my
check-writing privileges again.

The first time it happened was when all our utility checks bounced and they cut off our phone. Since I'm not good at subtraction, I had rounded off every check amount on the stubs. For example, if the check was for $5.17, I made the stub $6.00. I thought it was a good idea, because it was easy to subtract, and I was actually saving money. After I'd written quite a few checks, I figured I had saved at least ten dollars, so I bought one or two extra things. But instead of saving, we ended up having to borrow fifty dollars from his folks to cover the bad checks.

After a few months he let me try again. I was so careful. I used his calculator to subtract, and I knew my balance was perfect, right down to the last penny. When the dentist called and said our check to him had bounced, I called the bank and really spouted off about their incompetence.

"Did you subtract the service charge?" a sweet voice asked.

"What service charge?"

"On your statement." Frankly, I didn't know what she was talking about.

"You know," she said kindly, "the blue-and-white sheet that comes with your canceled checks."

"Oh, that. I thought the bank just used that to wrap the checks in."

"Oh, my, no!" She sounded choked. "You really should reconcile your statement." I hung up and wondered how I was going to reconcile my husband.

It's midnight, and after a few tears and quite a bit of shouting, it turned out that when I made the house payment I'd forgotten to write it in the check record. It seems to me anyone could have made an error like that. But why did it have to be me?

23

". . . Turn in the account of your stewardship, for you can no longer be steward" (Luke 16:2).

It's great to be able to give a good account to our husbands. Think what a joy it will be if we can give a good account of our stewardship to the Lord.

DIETING

I'M SO DISCOURAGED THIS MORNING THAT if there was any place open I'd go get a hot fudge sundae. I've been on this diet for two weeks and I've only lost three pounds. I lost those the first week and not an ounce since. I didn't eat one thing yesterday that wasn't on the diet except one dinky toasted marshmallow — and a very small chunk of cheese. Oh, yes, and half a peanut butter sandwich. Right now I'm having ugly thoughts about being slender and glamorous. Who cares? I mean, really, who wants to look like a model on television? *I* do!

But I'll never be slender. No matter what happens to me, I still have a tremendous appetite. Some people get the flu and throw up; but when I get the flu, I crave pecan pie. Nothing ever spoils my appetite. I've never even had morning sickness. How I wish I could get so skinny that people would *urge* me to eat.

There's too much emphasis today on being thin. Dress designers must have it in for us chubbies. Why can't they design some styles where the skinny girls would have to pad *their* waistlines so they'd look as glamorous as the rest of us? We are so gullible, and we fall for anything that's supposed to be in style, so why not have some "fat" propaganda? We could have mottoes like "Bulges Are Back!" or "Inches Are In." Or how about "Find Freedom in Fat!"

Of course, I know extra pounds shorten one's life, but if I'm going to have to diet all my life, do I really want to prolong it?

I'm so hungry right now I'm on the verge of a splurge. I've got to get my mind off food. I read an article the other day that said most of the trouble with food is in the head anyway, and to get busy either with work or a hobby. My hobby is making fudge — old-fashioned cocoa fudge with walnuts, or chocolate chip with marshmallow, or divinity, or peanut butter fudge. . . .

What time is it anyway? Only nine-thirty, and I can't have anything until noon. Then I get a cup of boullion and two lettuce leaves. I think I'll eat one of those lettuce leaves now, garnished with lunch meat and a little mayonnaise. After all, if I get too discouraged, I'll go off my diet.

"But I keep under my body, and bring it into subjection" (1 Cor. 9:27 KJV).

If we turn to the Lord before we open the refrigerator door, He will help us keep it closed.

DECISIONS

"CAN'T MAKE UP YOUR MIND?" MARY SAID, after we had looked at blouses for over an hour. She leaned against a counter and tried not to look tired.

"Isn't it awful?" I apologized. "I really need a new blouse for the Ladies Retreat, but there are so many decisions! Should I get long sleeves or short, an over-blouse or one to tuck in, print or plain? It drives me crazy!"

"Let's try the process of elimination," she suggested. "First, what price range?"

"Hmmm. Well, probably no more than — still, I only get — "

"How about ten dollars?"

"Okay."

"Then we will only look at these two racks. Now, what will you be wearing it with?" And so, by her method, we figured out what style and colors would be best. At last we found two blouses that exactly met all requirements, but I still went home empty-handed. I couldn't decide whether to get the plain one or the striped.

On the following Saturday my husband asked, "Do you want any vegetables from the garden this morning?"

27

"I sure do," I answered sweetly.

"What kind? Zucchini? Carrots? Beets?"

"Hmmm. Let me think."

He stood there waiting. After a moment of silence, he groaned, "Come on, honey. I want to start watering."

"Well — I just can't decide in one minute what we're going to eat all weekend. If mother comes over I'll want to serve zucchini, but if not — probably — " He was gone.

Later, when he came back in for coffee, I said, "I've made up my mind — just bring in some squash and carrots. We've had beets a lot lately."

"How many?"

"Oh. Let me think. It depends on the size." He folded his arms and leaned against the counter. "If they're big — still, I can always — maybe . . ." I compressed my lips and tried to think, but he walked out on me. That really irritated me. I wonder how he'd feel if I walked out on him?

Maybe I should just go shopping again — I still haven't bought a blouse for Ladies Retreat — but then I'd have to do my work this afternoon. Or should I put it off until Monday?

"Then we will be no longer infants, tossed back and forth by the waves, and blown here and there by every wind of teaching . . ." (Eph. 4:14).

Sometimes it's hard to know exactly what we want — but we should be able to tell exactly what we believe: Christ died for our sins.

NEW YEAR'S RESOLUTIONS

LAST NEW YEAR'S, AFTER I HAD VOWED TO go on a diet, and then gained three pounds by January 5th, I said I'd never again make a New Year's resolution. But my marriage is at stake. My husband dropped a jar of mustard this evening, and it broke all over the floor, just because I hadn't screwed the cap all the way on.

"You do so many *tacky* things," he grumbled as he mopped mustard off his shoes and pants. I know it's true. So, starting in the morning, I resolve to "Quit Doing Tacky Things," such as:

1. I vow to put away my groceries before the frozen foods thaw.

2. No more stirring coffee with the sugar spoon.

3. I promise not to mend things with the wrong color thread because I'm too lazy to change the bobbin.

4. Never again will I wear a dress with the hem stapled in.

5. If a slip is too long, I'll shorten it instead of tucking it up in my bra.

6. No more putting dishes in the cupboard without drying them — at least on the bottom.

29

7. I vow I will not hang my clothes on chairs and doorknobs, nor will I hang them up wrong-side-out.

8. I will get a box for rubber bands instead of shooting them in the air.

9. I will not put away a Tupperware container without its lid.

10. New toilet paper will go on the roller as soon as I unwrap it, instead of when it's half used.

There. I feel better already. Now if I can just find a thumbtack to put these resolutions up where I can read them. . . . Maybe this big safety pin will do.

"It is better that you should not vow than that you should vow and not pay" (Eccl. 5:5).

If we can recognize our faults we've made progress; but let's not make vows unless we're willing to make changes.

OBEDIENCE

WE WERE PLANNING OUR VACATION, AND I was really excited, until I remembered Tummy, our seventy-pound Labrador pup who thinks he is our son.

"Could we leave him with your mother?" my husband asked.

"I don't think she could take it for two whole weeks," I answered.

"Well, we could take him along, provided you train him."

"What do you mean? He's already housebroken."

"Obedience," he answered. "Having him come when he's called. Staying in the car without barking."

I doubted my ability to teach him obedience, because he got me trained first. But I decided to call my good friend who has an obedient poodle. I explained the problem.

"Get a choker chain and a leash," she advised. "He'll soon learn he has to come when you give it a tug. And start taking him in the car so he'll get used to travel."

I looked down at Tummy, our adorable, outdoor dog, asleep at my feet.

"Tummy, want to go to the store?" He woke up and

31

raised his head. One ear was wrong side out. "Come on, sweetie! Let's go." I started for the door, but he only stared at me. "*Come!*" I said sternly. He rolled over on his back and thumped his tail apologetically. I had to carry him to the car, and when I opened the door, he stiffened all four legs. It was like trying to put an armload of assorted two-by-fours in the back seat. He shivered and slobbered all the way to the store.

I put the new chain around his neck, and when I got home I gave the leash a couple of jerks; but he dug his toenails into the upholstery and refused to come out.

"Good grief," I moaned. "Can I take two weeks of carrying him in and out of motels?"

At the end of a week, wearing his collar and leash, he would trot alongside me in the backyard with only an occasional yelp or gasp for breath, but my ankles looked as though I had some dread disease, because he switched sides about every fourth step.

Sadly, he hasn't learned to come when called, but only when we shout, "Stay!"

———— ∽◦∾ ————

"Has the LORD as great delight in burnt offerings and sacrifices, as in obeying the voice of the LORD? . . . To obey is better than sacrifice . . . " (1 Sam. 15:22).

"And being found in appearance as a man, [Christ] humbled himself and became obedient to death — even death on a cross!" (Phil. 2:8).

For our sakes Christ Jesus obeyed God. Let's make every effort, for *His* sake, also to obey God.

NO CHANGE

MY SISTER-IN-LAW, WHO IS A TERRIFIC cook, spent a few days with us. One morning she said authoritatively,

"Today I'm going to plan and cook all the meals, so you can rest."

"Wonderful!" I yelled. "I hate to cook." I went to the living room and picked up a book.

Pretty soon she called, "What do you use to mix eggs for scrambling?"

"A fork?" I guessed.

"Really? Hmm." I began to read again.

In a minute she shouted, "Where is your jar opener?"

"You mean can opener?" I got up and went to the kitchen. She was holding a jar of peaches.

"Don't you have one of those things you clamp on the jar and twist?" I took the jar from her, ran hot water on it, pounded it with a knife, and finally got it open. Nothing to it.

"Breakfast's ready!" she called after a little while. We all gaped at her beautiful, fluffy scrambled eggs, broiled peach halves, and melba toast.

After breakfast I took her to the store, but she wouldn't let me see what she bought. Before lunch she asked me,

"Where are your measuring cups and spoons?"

I had once owned measuring spoons, but where were they now?

"I don't have any," I admitted, embarrassed. "But you'll find a measuring cup in the sugar canister." She looked stunned, but lunch was delicious — shrimp Newburg and a squash casserole.

Before dinner she asked where I kept my spices. I showed her the salt, pepper, cinnamon, and chili powder.

"Don't you have any marjoram?" I shook my head. "I'm not sure what my veal scallopini will be like without marjoram." She looked around the kitchen. "Where is the food chopper?" Quickly, I pointed to the blender. "No, no," she said. "Don't you have a gadget" — she motioned up and down — "that dices food?" She sighed at my blank look. "Never mind. I'll use a knife." After awhile she came into the living room.

"I've looked everywhere for the potato masher."

I giggled.

"Don't you ever have mashed potatoes?"

"Of course. But I use instant."

The next day at the shopping center she handed me a bulging sack.

"These are for you, honey. No wonder you don't like to cook. You don't have anything to work with."

I don't know what to do with all these new measuring spoons, stir-things, and mashers. It's a cinch I'll never use them.

"Therefore, if any one is in Christ, he is a new creation;

the old has passed away, behold, the new has come" (2 Cor. 5:17 RSV).

" . . . just as Christ was raised from the dead through the glory of the Father, we too may live a new life" (Rom. 6:4).

Old habits are hard to get rid of, but when we surrender to Christ, old things *do* pass away, and we do live a new life.

SEW SEW

OUR VARIETY STORE HAS JUST RECEIVED a lot of new yard goods. The bolts of material are piled high, and beautiful prints in brilliant colors are swagged from hanging rings. All the mannequins are dressed up in new patterns, and everything is on sale! While I was walking up and down the aisles touching the material, my heart began to beat faster. I picked up a bolt of yellow polyester and looked around for a clerk.

"I can save so much money!" I thought. "I'll try it one more time."

"Don't be an idiot," a voice within me whispered, and I put the bolt down. I made myself walk out of the store, muttering to myself,

"You are not a seamstress; you have never been a seamstress; you will never be a seamstress."

Heaven knows I've tried. I have a drawer full of the pitiful scraps of my failures. There is the bright green, silky material that should have made a stunning dress. I was doing fine on it until I got the sleeves in upside down. They were puffed sleeves, and although I could have gotten used to the tightness across my shoulders, I could never get used to those bags under my arms. I wore the dress a few times, but I always felt self-conscious. I would sort of push back into the sofa and put throw pillows over my arms.

I almost cry when I look at the leftover pink velvet I used to make my daughter a long, flower-girl dress. Velvet is so sneaky. Even after the seams were basted, they wouldn't come out even, and I had to keep trimming them, which made the skirt sort of uneven. And I made the mistake of placing some of the pattern pieces upside down on the velvet. Due to the uneven hemline and the way the light hit the upside-down pieces, my little girl looked like she was in a scalloped awning the night of the wedding.

There are some pieces of black velveteen left from what I had hoped would be a glamorous pantsuit, but I had trouble with the zipper in the pants. The first time I tried them on the front looked beautiful, but the zipper tab was on the inside. I would have left it, but I couldn't get my hand in to zip it up, and I knew it wouldn't look right with a string attached to the tab. After taking the zipper out and putting it in three times, the whole zipper area looked like I had worn the pants for an acupuncture treatment.

A piece of blue nylon pops out every time I open the drawer. It is a beautiful shade of blue and I thought I'd be beautiful too, in a dress with gathers at the waist. But the material wouldn't drape, and I looked like a fat ballerina the only time I wore it.

I have a friend who is an excellent seamstress. She keeps saying, "You'll learn!" Maybe she's right. Maybe I'll go to the store this afternoon and browse around.

<hr />

"She seeks wool and flax, and works with willing hands

. . . all her household are clothed in scarlet. She makes herself coverings . . ." (Prov. 31:13,21,22).

"I can do everything through him who gives me strength" (Phil. 4:13).

As homemakers, some things we try to do aren't easy, but if we remember to ask Him for help, we *can* do them.

COUNTESS OF SANDWICH

ONE THING I HATE TO DO IS MAKE lunches. It seems as if I've been making sandwiches for a hundred and two years. When I was only eight, my sister said, "Starting Monday you'll have to make your own lunch — you're old enough."

Usually all we had to make sandwiches of was peanut butter. But I loved peanut butter, and I invented many variations. Some of my favorites were peanut butter and mustard, peanut butter and mashed pinto beans, peanut butter and dill pickles. Peanut butter and catsup isn't bad, especially if you're out of margarine or jelly.

Sometimes, when there was no peanut butter, I'd have to scramble an egg. By lunchtime the bread and waxed paper would be steamed together in a soggy mess.

Occasionally there would be a real crisis — no bread. I've made sandwiches from crackers, cornbread, and even cold biscuits. Once, when my sister was in high school, she cried herself to sleep because her lunch sack split, and her biscuit sandwiches rolled and bounced down the hall like tennis balls, in front of her boyfriend.

When I got married, I thought it would be the gateway to

freedom, but I found I still had to pack lunches. Except that my husband didn't like peanut butter sandwiches. He wanted salami. After about a year, though, he told me he didn't want salami every day. So I tried to brighten up his lunch with some of his favorite foods, like sandwiches made with leftover spaghetti and meatballs. I thought he'd love them, but he suggested I put him back on salami.

When our children got to be school age, there were more sandwiches to make and different tastes to satisfy. For example, my son will not eat cold liver sandwiches.

I was looking forward to the time when the children would be grown and married and my husband would retire, and then — oh happy day — no more lunch making. But my mother said,

"No, honey, you'll still be making lunches, and *he'll* be there to eat them."

<hr>

"Then Jesus declared, 'I am the bread of life. He who comes to me will never go hungry, and he who believes in me will never be thirsty" (John 6:35).

Homemakers have always had to make lunches — but feeding on the Bread of Life before breakfast makes the job easier.

NAME TAGS

WOULDN'T IT BE GREAT IF IT WAS THE custom for everyone to wear name tags at all times? I get so embarrassed when I can't remember people's names. I might know where they work, how many children they have, and what church they go to, but their names by-pass my mind.

Introductions are the worst. I mean, when I'm supposed to introduce one person to another, even the names of people I've known for years sometimes disappear through the hole in my head.

"Please forgive me," I have to say, "but I can't remember your name." Long-standing friends look dumbfounded. Later, I notice, they are decidedly cool toward me.

At social gatherings I panic and try to avoid introductions. If I'm trapped, however, there are a few ruses that work pretty well.

If I'm the only person who can introduce two people, and I can't remember their names, I just start walking away and call over my shoulder,

"Will you two introduce yourselves? I'm late!"

Something else that works pretty well is to keep talking to both people, and if they look embarrassed or ill at ease I say, "Oh, don't you know each other? Well, I'll just let you two get acquainted." Then I scurry away to talk to someone whose name I remember.

If I think I can get away with it, sometimes I look first at one and then the other and say,

"Introduce me, okay?" That puts the burden on *them*, and *they* have to say, "I'm sorry, I've forgotten your name."

I guess I'm not alone in this problem. I had a friend a few years ago (I can't think of her name), but anyway, I took some other friends over to see this woman's new baby.

"What's his name?" one of them asked.

My friend looked blank, then horrified, then her eyes filled with tears. She couldn't remember her own son's name.

Well, I'm not that bad off yet. But my kids have strict orders to keep their name tags *on*.

———— ⋙⋘ ————

". . . that you may know that it is I, the LORD, the God of Israel who call you by your name" (Isa. 45:3).

We forget names, and sometimes we even forget God; but He never forgets us, and He calls us by name!

LATE AGAIN

WHEN I GOT TO THE LOCKED CHOIR room last Sunday, and Mary had to come back to let me in and help me find my robe, and I barely made it into the choir loft with the rest of the group, I promised myself that I would never be late again. (I have promised that before.)

I'm always running late and I don't know why. I read an article once which stated that people who are habitually late have a subconscious desire to speed. Could I have a secret compulsion to be a race driver? My husband says I only have two speeds — stop and floorboard. But that's not true. I only speed when I'm late, which is most of the time. I don't understand it. I always allow myself plenty of time to get ready. But there does seem to be a tendency on my part to take on extra projects when I have the least time.

Sunday morning I had forgotten to take a roast out of the freezer, so I decided to make spaghetti and meatballs. The hamburger was frozen too, and it took extra time to run hot water on it and chisel off bits with the paring knife until it was soft enough to shape into balls.

Also, I have this problem of thinking I can do more in a

certain time that I can. For years I've kept my kitchen clock seven minutes fast, but this trick doesn't work any more. "I can whip up this cake mix before I have to leave," I tell myself, "because the clock is fast."

My habitual tardiness is one reason I changed churches. One morning I was late (again) to my old church; and rather than be embarrassed, I stopped at my present church, because it's much closer to home. But I *must not* start being late again, because there's no other church closer.

Most of my family is resigned to the fact that if I say eleven o'clock I will arrive at eleven-thirty. However, my husband won't put up with me, and once he even drove off without me. (That's why I keep a comb, hairspray, nail polish, and lipstick in the glove compartment.)

How can I be sure I won't be late next Sunday? I think I'll set two alarms, twenty minutes apart. Then when the second one goes off. . . .

"Look carefully then how you walk, not as unwise men but as wise, making the most of the time . . ." (Eph. 5:15,16 RSV).

"And be kind to one another . . ." (Eph. 4:32 RSV).

If we could realize that always being late is not only foolish but unkind, then we could take the problem to the Lord. He will give us the determination to be on time.

OPEN UP!

LAST NIGHT AFTER I SWEPT UP THE FRO-zen peas, I had to face the fact that I'm definitely sub-normal when it comes to opening things. I suspected it when as a young girl I could never do a simple thing like taking the paraffin off a glass without rocketing a blob of jelly up to the ceiling. I don't know what my problem is, but directions like "Run thumbnail along dotted line and lift cover" always end with a broken fingernail and food on the floor. If it says "Pull tab," the tab comes off in my hand. If it says "Snip corner," I squirt sauce all over the stove. And meat! I can never get the hamburger out until I've torn the plastic to shreds.

This morning I even had trouble opening the milk carton. There were those words *To open,* with a sly little arrow pointing inside; so with teeth clenched and eyes squinting, I carefully pulled it apart. "Push up" was the next instruction, but even with both hands I could not push it up. I decided to cut the wax loose with a knife and that's how I cut my thumb. As expensive as milk is I cried quite a bit over the amount I spilled.

I have trouble with spray cans, too. On the oven cleaner

I just bought, there's a little plastic tab over the nozzle that reads: "Do not remove. Lift tab." I don't know what to do. It's obvious, even to me, that in order to use the stuff I will have to get that tab out of the way. But it says "Do not remove." I don't want to break a law or something. Well, I won't worry about it. I didn't want to clean the oven anyway.

I never seem to be able to open anything by directions. The oatmeal, powdered sugar, crackers, and cereals in my cupboards all look like they were damaged in shipment.

Tonight I plan to have canned ham, but I dread opening it. I know the key will come off the metal strip and I'll end up having to pull the strip off with pliers. I also plan to have some frozen peas again. But I'm not about to be fooled by that "Pull strip along perforated edge" instruction. I'm going out to the garage and get my husband's hatchet.

"Now the body is not made up of one part but of many. . . . But in fact God has arranged the parts in the body, every one of them, just as he wanted them to be" (1 Cor. 12:14,18).

"Those parts of the body that seem to be weaker are indispensable" (1 Cor. 12:22).

No matter how inept or incompetent we think we are, God has placed us in the body of Christ and declares us necessary!

DOOR TO POOR

"GOOD MORNING!" THE GOOD-LOOKING
fellow at the door exuded personality. "I wonder if you'd
be interested in some Grade A, T-bone steaks?"

I was on guard because a few days before my husband
had given me a long sermon about buying from door-to-
door salesmen.

"According to this article, their stuff is usually inferior,
misrepresented, or overpriced," he admonished.

"What about Girl Scout cookies and other good
causes?"

He put his hands up.

"All right. But I'm telling you that with prices the way
they are you'd better think about *our* cause. We're barely
making ends meet."

"Are you saying not to buy *anything* at the door?"

"No. But buy only what you need and what is obviously
a good buy."

"This is a good buy," the good-looking man said. "You
see, my company usually sells only to hotels and better
restaurants, but today they find they have a few boxes of
steaks on hand that they'd like to dump quickly." He

named a price for twenty-five T-bone steaks. He showed them to me, and they were beautiful.

As I hesitated he added, "Your neighbor bought twenty-five." That settled it.

That night I led my hubby to the freezer and waited for praise. He didn't say anything, but pulled out a pad and pencil. Quickly he showed me that I had paid over a dollar a pound more than I would have at our market.

"Besides that," he added, "what makes you think we can afford to eat T-bones?" There were several more "besides thats" and I finally promised I would never, never buy from the door again.

I don't know whether to show him these Boy Scout donuts or eat them all myself.

* * *

"So the men partook of their provisions, and did not ask direction from the LORD" (Josh. 9:14).

"In all your ways acknowledge him, and he will make straight your paths" (Prov. 3:6).

If we remember to pray first, we probably won't regret our actions later.

A MOVING EXPERIENCE

IN THE MAIL I RECEIVED A CARD FROM A friend. "We're moving into a home of our own," she wrote. "We're so excited." I said a little prayer for her, knowing the mess she would be in.

When we moved, another friend expressed similar feelings for me.

"I don't envy you," she said. "You won't be able to find anything for weeks."

"Au contraire!" I said. "I have a plan." I hoped I didn't sound smug, but I was positive this move wouldn't be as chaotic as our previous ones. "We'll be settled in three days."

The plan was simple. As I packed things in boxes I took care to mark them with a black felt-tip pen:

COOKING UTENSILS — KITCHEN

MEDICINE, HEATING PAD, ETC. — BATHROOM

DISHES, GLASSES — KITCHEN

Why should there be any confusion?

On moving day I said to one of the movers, "I've labeled all the boxes, so you'll know where to put them." Either he didn't understand me, or else he couldn't read, because when I arrived at the new house all the boxes were stacked in the kitchen. It looked like a supermarket storeroom.

I took a huge box off the first stack and discovered it was full of trash from the old house. The next box said SOAP, CLEANING SUPPLIES, ETC. — SERVICE PORCH. I couldn't get to the porch so I put it alongside the trash box in the living room.

By late afternoon I had moved most of the boxes out of the kitchen and into every other room in the house. In spite of the labels I couldn't find many things I needed — like the spatula to turn hamburgers that night. (I learned that a metal shoehorn can be used if necessary.)

After dinner I had to get the beds made.

"Has anyone seen a box marked LINENS?" I yelled.

There was no response. They were all too busy trying to get their own things straightened out. When I packed, by the time I got to the bedrooms, I had run out of boxes, so in a flash of inspiration I had dumped the contents of bureau drawers onto the bedspreads and tied them up like bunches of laundry.

About the fourth day my friend called.

"Well, how did your plan work?" She would have to ask.

I sat down on a box marked KEEPSAKES — GARAGE, and put my feet up on another box labeled SHOES, RAINCOATS, ETC. — HALL CLOSET.

"The best laid schemes —" I quoted Robert Burns.

"A man's pride will bring him low . . ." (Prov. 29:23).

"Do you see a man who is hasty in his words? There is more hope for a fool than for him" (Prov. 29:20).

Just when we think we are the smartest, we find out differently. And wonder of wonders, God uses us anyway.

KID STUFF

MY SISTER HURT MY FEELINGS THE other day about how I'm raising my kids. I doubt that my children will turn out to be gangsters any more than hers. I won't be leaving them in her care again — she said so.

"Your children don't know the meaning of the word *no,*" she complained. She's all for beating on them to make them mind.

Evidently the first thing that happened that day was when she took them with her to the drugstore and my three-year-old picked up a gallon of wine and dropped it. Sis said the whole place smelled like Busch Gardens, and she had to pay four dollars for it. Of course I'll pay her back when I can afford it, even though I'd rather not spend my money on liquor.

Later, at her house, one of the kids (and I'll bet hers were in on it too) spilled a whole bottle of her favorite cologne. Frankly, I'm not too crazy about that scent, and I'll be glad when it wears off my daughter's Pooh bear.

I guess the last thing that upset her was when my children began to fight over her movie camera. Why would she be dopey enough to leave it low enough for the kids to reach? Anyway, she said they got to running through the house; the front screen was locked when they burst through it; and they landed in a heap on the front porch. I tried to glue the cover back on the camera, but I think she'll have to get plastic glue before it will stick. She hasn't found the cartridge yet. It went flying through the air, and unfortunately no one noticed where it landed. I am sorry about that. She had taken some good shots of my kids at the family picnic on the Fourth.

Down in my heart I think my sister is probably right about the little characters. Maybe they will turn out to be hoodlums. I'm half afraid of them myself.

"Do not withhold discipline from a child; if you beat him with a rod, he will not die. If you beat him with the rod, you will save his life from Sheol" (Prov. 23:13,14).

"Children, obey your parents in the Lord, for this is right" (Eph. 6:1).

No one will want to be around our children if they won't obey. And they won't obey without some application of the rod of discipline.

FARMER'S WIFE

REMEMBER THE OLD SAYING, "YOU CAN take the boy out of the country, but you can't take the country out of the boy"? Well, it works both ways. I'm a city girl who never saw a real cow until I was ten, and although we've lived on this half acre for four years, I'll never learn how to be a farmer's wife.

Of course I'm not a real farmer's wife. I don't have to slop hogs or milk cows. But I do have to feed chickens and pheasants, gather eggs, tend to incubators, and clean out brooders, plus do *something* with Farmer G's green beans, beets, carrots, apricots, plums, and spinach.

Take green beans. (Oh, I wish you could!) There is a certain skill and rhythm to "snapping" green beans. For my city sisters who thought green beans came from freezers, this means breaking off both the ends, then snapping them into pieces about an inch and a half long. It's not an unpleasant chore, and can be done while talking to someone or watching television. The skill comes in being coordinated enough not to put the ends in with the good parts. I was enjoying a TV variety show the other night, and I had my lap full of beans on a towel, a big pan on the coffee table in front of me, and a paper sack on the floor. The "snick-snick" as I snapped off the ends, then "flap" as the ends landed in the bag, then the "snap-snap — clunk" as the beans hit the pan, made a pleasant background to the music. Suddenly I realized the sound was "snick-snick-clunk" and then "snap-snap-flap." It took an extra ten minutes to get all the ends out of the good pieces and rescue the beans from the bag.

Then there are beets. Did you know you aren't supposed to peel them before you cook them? I didn't. Pale brown beets do not have much eye-appeal, and even a cup of bleach hasn't completely taken away the pink tinge from my sink.

Everything I've served lately seems to turn off my family's appetite. I think it's because I'm trying so hard not to waste anything. Does liver and cabbage balls sound so bad? I can't help but get my feelings hurt when they won't even taste my innovations. And I'd like to meet the fellow who first said, "easy as pie." I have never made an easy pie — nor a good pie, even when I used pancake flour.

I wish old MacDonald had *this* farm. I've sort of got my eye on a high-rise apartment.

"And do not grumble, as some of them did — and were killed by the destroying angel" (1 Cor. 10:10).

" . . . and my people shall be satisfied with my goodness, says the LORD" (Jer. 31:14).

When we complain and dwell on our problems, it's probably because we haven't taken time to dwell on His goodness.

ROLLERS AND ROBE

MY HUSBAND HAD BARELY LEFT FOR work one morning when he telephoned.

"Honey, I left some blueprints on the table by my chair. Would you jump in the car and bring them to me?"

"Sure," I answered. "But it'll be a little while before I can dress and comb my hair."

"Don't take time for that, hon. I need them right now — we're in a meeting."

"Okay. I'll dress as quickly as I can."

"Do you have to dress? Aren't you in your robe?"

"Yes — but I look awful. My hair is in rollers and I don't have my face on."

"That's okay. I'll meet you in the parking lot. Nobody will see you. Please hurry." He hung up.

He was waiting for me in the parking lot, and as I stopped beside him, a good-looking man came out of the building and hurried over to us.

"Oh, no!" I murmured.

"Honey, this is a new employee. I'd like you to meet Ed Taylor."

"So this is your little lady," Ed said and chuckled. I was so mortified I could barely say "Pleased to meet you." I handed over the blueprints and put the car in drive.

"Wait a minute," he said. "Where's that little green slip of paper?"

"I didn't see any slip of paper," I said. Mr. Taylor just stood there grinning. My husband unrolled the prints and shook them.

"It was clipped on. It must have come off. Get out of the car a minute, would you? It may be under the seat."

I got out of the car in my old, faded, tiger-print robe with one button missing. The green slip of paper fluttered down and stuck in the edge of one bedroom slipper. I bent over to get it and a curler fell out on the pavement. Wouldn't this nightmare ever end? I got back in the car and Ed said,

"It's been nice to meet you! Hope to see you again."

Seeing him again was the last thing I wanted.

A funny thing happened, though, at the company picnic. I was dressed in a darling new outfit, and my hair turned out extra special that day. This same Ed Taylor came over to our table and my husband said, "Ed, you remember my wife?"

He looked at me blankly.

"No, I've never had the pleasure."

Neither of us corrected him.

~·~

"Humble yourselves before the Lord, and he will lift you up" (James 4:10).

"I, I am he who blots out your transgressions for my own sake, and I will not remember your sins" (Isa. 43:25).

Unfortunately, we cannot forget our blunders and sins. But if we confess our sins, God *forgets* them!

56

VACATION BIBLE SCHOOL

WE JUST FINISHED VACATION BIBLE SCHOOL and I served as "helper" in the third and fourth grades. I doubt that the director thought of me as "helper" though, due to a series of incidents that could have done lasting damage to several little souls.

I was supposed to help in the daily memory work. The Bible verses were printed in large letters, cut up into phrases, and backed by flannel. The whole verse was supposed to be put on the flannelboard first, then pieces were taken down a few words at a time, until the children could say it without help. I never quite got the knack of putting the phrases up in the right order. For example, one day my version of the Twenty-third Psalm looked like this:

> THE LORD IS MY SHEPHERD
> IN GREEN PASTURES:
> HE LEADETH ME BESIDE
> I SHALL NOT WANT.

Quite often when I did have them on the board correctly, they would fall off and flutter across the room. Then there would be a tornado of children running after the pieces, leaping over chairs, grabbing each other's clothes, and screaming, in an effort to help me.

After most of the children learned the daily verse, I would take all the pieces away and see if they could recite it from memory. I would lead them in a loud, clear voice, and invariably I would say it wrong. What a miserable feeling to see all those little faces chirping out their Bible verse in unison, suddenly stop, look bewildered, and then slowly grin.

I thought I might be better at the handcraft, but I believe the macramé project was too hard for the children.

"Now watch, children," the lady in charge of handcraft shouted above thirty-two squirming kids, who were already pulling their yarn out of sacks and spilling nails and beads all over the tables.

"First we have to make this frame, and we'll have to take turns using the hammers." Hammers? I shuddered as I thought of those kids with lethal weapons in their hands.

All the children were anxious to drive their eight nails into the corners of their four pieces of wood, and of course they needed my help. But I can't drive a nail straight in the privacy of my home, much less with a ring of hammer-waving kids pressing in on me.

The day we had to use the yarn was my worst. The craft teacher showed us over and over how to make a square knot, and it did seem simple; but when I tried it, it always took the shape of a triangle. I excused myself to go to the rest room; but one little girl pleaded with me to help her, so we sat down on the floor and spread the multicolored yarn out in front of us. She didn't seem to know the difference, so I quickly made a series of triangle knots, but the teacher caught me and gave me a withering look.

"If a thing's worth doing," she quoted, "it's worth doing right." I had to untie all those knots while the little girl sat with her arms folded across her stomach.

At refreshment time I was to help get the youngsters lined up and keep them from demolishing the table. The kitchen helpers looked pretty grim about the three glasses of punch I spilled when I tried to keep some boys from crawling under the table. After that they insisted I rest during refreshment time.

The night of the program I was so proud of our group, even if I did lead them up on the stage at the wrong time. Their faces glowed with such an angelic light and the parents seemed so happy, I decided I'd help again next year — if they let me.

"... bring them up in the training and instruction of the Lord" (Eph. 6:4).

"And God hath set some in the church, first apostles, secondarily prophets, thirdly teachers, after that ... helps ..." (1 Cor. 12:28 KJV).

If we are willing, God can take our clumsy efforts and make them count.

CONSCIOUS OF MY CONSCIENCE

ANDREW, THE SON OF THE BEST HOUSE-keeper in the block, was standing in our driveway when I got home from the store.

"Need some help with your groceries?" he offered.

"Sure," I said and opened the trunk. There were four sacks, and we each carried in two. "Just put them on the counter." He walked over to it and then looked at me. I saw his problem. No room. Every inch of space from the wall to the sink was covered. There was a bottle of hand lotion, some unopened mail, a new roll of paper towels, the blender, two bars of soap, the cutting board, clean and dirty dishes, a box of Bran Buds, nutcrackers, and a portable radio. The toaster, more dirty dishes, cleanser, potholders, liquid soap, a loaf of bread, the butter dish, and a hammer were on the other side of the sink.

"I'm sorry, Andrew." (Why hadn't I listened to my conscience and straightened up the house before going to the store?) "Just put them on the table." He moved quickly to the table and again turned and looked at me. This was humiliating. In the center was a large bouquet of wilted roses. Actually they were dried. The vase was surrounded by books, folded bath towels, several coffee cups, the bank statement with its checks spread out, a Barbie doll, and Play-doh — in all colors.

"This is quite a mess, isn't it?" I spoke as though we were in someone else's house. He nodded solemnly.

"I know!" I exclaimed. "Put them out on the washing machine —" I looked around him and saw that the washing machine and dryer were piled high with mounds of dirty clothes (I planned to wash), a basket of tomatoes (I planned to can), a gallon of bleach, grass cutters, a pair of mud-crusted tennis shoes, and a bottle of Windex.

"Well, Andrew," I giggled with embarrassment, "just put them on the floor." I leaned over and put down my two sacks. I found the cookie jar on top of the refrigerator behind several egg cartons, a box I was saving, a Thermos bottle, and the teapot, and let him help himself.

When he was gone, I looked around the house. Every flat surface — tables, TV, bureaus — had something on it. Even the chairs were covered with magazines, toys, or clothes.

"Is there something to be learned from this?" I asked myself.

"Yes, clod," I answered back. "You're lazy, slipshod, and incompetent. You should be ashamed and mend your ways!"

After that edict I not only put away the groceries, I put away everything on top of everything. The house looks nice, but I don't know where anything is, and I can't get the drawers open to look.

"All day long my disgrace is before me, and shame has covered my face" (Ps. 44:15).

"Now this is our boast: Our conscience testifies that we have conducted ourselves in the world . . . in the holiness and sincerity that are from God" (2 Cor. 1:12).

When we don't behave in a way to bring honor to Christ, we are ashamed. But oh! The *joy* of a clear conscience.

MONEYBAGS

I WONDER IF OTHER WOMEN HAVE AS much trouble with their purses as I do. I try to keep mine neat, but my keys, glasses, and billfold are always buried underneath a mess of tissue, cash register tapes, and make-up. I can't remember how many times I've had to dump everything out on the hood of my car before I could find the car keys.

A while back I decided I could whip the problem by getting a purse with three divisions. On one side I put my make-up, and on the other I put a notebook and keys. In the zippered part I put my billfold, checkbook, and credit cards. It was so neat. That lasted until the checkbook got caught and I had to break the zipper to get it open.

I quit trying to be neat for a while, and then my husband gave me an elegant black leather bag for Christmas. It closed with a flap over the top, fastened with an eyelet that buttoned on a little brass knob. From the start I had trouble with that knob. It's so humiliating to be at the checkout counter during rush hour, unable to open your own purse. I finally twisted the brass thing off, and then got a shoulder bag. Women who carry them look so chic and carefree; I was sure that was what I needed. It would leave both hands free to put my things away neatly.

The first day I used my shoulder bag I went to the shopping center. I hopped out of the car and slung the strap over my shoulder; I felt younger and more carefree already. I started walking at a brisk pace and stumbled over my new bag. The dumb thing had slid off my shoulder and tripped me. I glanced around to see if anyone had witnessed this idiotic feat, then picked it up, put the strap firmly back on my shoulder, and set off again. Down it went. Evidently I couldn't walk and carry it at the same time. I took a few more cautious steps and learned if I pushed down hard on the bag it would stay in place. That evening I was worn out from pushing down on my purse and pulling up on the strap. I guess my shoulders aren't as square as they should be . . . or maybe those women aren't as carefree as they look.

Stylists are trying to get men to carry shoulder bags, but why should they be encumbered with a bag when they have all those pockets? I'm looking for pants right now with four pockets in them. I could keep my make-up in one back pocket, my billfold and checkbook in the other, and my keys and credit cards in the front. I guess I could keep my glasses on.

". . . let us throw off every thing that hinders and the sin that so easily entangles . . . " (Heb. 12:1).

"But Martha was distracted by all the preparations. . . . 'Martha, Martha,' the Lord answered, 'you are worried and upset about many things' " (Luke 10:40,41).

A cluttered purse is irritating and embarrassing, but how about lives that get so cluttered Christ is crowded out?

CAUGHT!

TODAY WAS THE DAY I HAD PLANNED TO start painting the kitchen cupboards; and feeling reasonably well organized, I decided to put a stew in the crock pot. While I painted, dinner would be cooking. But I didn't have any onions.

"You won't believe," my neighbor said over the phone, "but I'm out of onions, too."

I looked down at my old, black, paint-spattered slacks and baggy plaid shirt that used to be my husband's and wondered if I dared go to the store in that get-up. My hair was flat and straight, and I wasn't wearing make-up. But if I took time to clean up, I might get out of the mood for painting. But what if I would run into someone I know? I decided to take the chance. I grabbed my purse, got into the car, and put on my sunglasses. If they could disguise Hollywood stars maybe they would hide me.

In the store I got a basket, knowing it was emotionally impossible for me to buy only an onion, and started up and down the aisles. I knew it! At the frozen foods I met the Sunday school superintendent, all dressed up for a luncheon.

"I've been meaning to call you about some visual aids," she said. "We could discuss it over coffee" — her eyes kept flitting from my pants to my shirt and back to my face — "but maybe this wouldn't be a good time." I told her about the cupboards and hurried on.

In the next aisle I recognized the profile of one of the ladies in the library. I turned the basket around so fast it almost turned over. I skittered away as quickly as I could, and just as I turned the corner I bumped my basket head-on into my former pastor's basket.

"Excuse me," I mumbled, starting away and hoping my dark glasses would hide me.

"Hey there," he said. "Not so fast! We've been missing you."

What could be worse? Caught in this disreputable outfit and now I would have to explain why I had changed churches. Could I get away with mistaken identity?

"Hi there, pastor," I said, pressing into my basket.

"Well, well, it's nice to see you once more," he said, and I looked down at my hole-infested tennis shoes, "before I leave town," he continued.

"Leave?"

"Yes, I've been transferred to the Valley. In fact, we're moving today. That's why I have on this miserable outfit." There were several blobs of paint on his pants, too.

"God bless you," I said, grinning.

I put a few onions in a sack, got in line, and took off my sunglasses.

" . . . and be sure your sin will find you out" (Num. 32:23).

"If we confess our sins, he is faithful and just and will forgive us our sins and purify us from all unrighteousness" (1 John 1:9).

It's embarrassing to meet acquaintances in our worst clothes, but how awful it would be to meet Jesus with our sins unconfessed.

FUN AND SHAMES

ED AND KAY WERE OVER LAST NIGHT TO play Monopoly. Finally, after I had to sell all my houses and mortgage my property, I quit and went into the kitchen to fix refreshments.

I made cocoa, fried bacon, and then made open-faced, grilled cheese sandwiches. Tastefully, I arranged the four plates, napkins, mugs of hot chocolate (with marshmallows), and a big bowl of potato chips on a large tray. Taking small steps and being extremely careful I made my way to the living room and approached the card table. The tray was heavy and my wrists were beginning to ache.

"I thought you'd be through by now," I said. "The refreshments are ready."

"Good," Kay said. "I'm tired of this game." She quickly put her houses and cards in the box. The two fellows shrugged and put their things away. Before my husband moved the box off the table, I took a step forward. I don't know what happened. Maybe I stumbled or maybe my wrists just gave out, but I pitched the tray at the table, and hot cocoa and potato chips went everywhere.

Kay looked down at the brown puddle in her lap and

then yelled. She leaped up and the table lurched into Ed's stomach. He pushed it back and then pulled his hand up. It was draped with melted cheese and hundred-dollar bills. They both looked horror-stricken.

My husband looked up at me with wild eyes and his mouth open. As well as he knows me, he couldn't believe this was happening. I couldn't believe it either. The potato chips were soggy and purple and the once appetizing sandwiches looked like garbage. In the silence, we all became aware of a drip, drip, drip as the remains of the cocoa oozed over the table and onto the carpet.

This morning I got to thinking how well it all turned out. In the first place, not one of us needed those extra calories at bedtime; and secondly, I cleaned the cocoa spots so well that my husband is going to shampoo the whole carpet tonight, to match the clean areas. Thirdly, I was getting tired of Monopoly.

<hr>

"Give thanks in all circumstances, for this is God's will for you in Christ Jesus" (1 Thess. 5:18).

It's hard to be thankful at the time, but usually today's disasters turn into tomorrow's blessings.

DARN THOSE SOCKS

THE OTHER NIGHT WHILE WE WERE watching TV, I noticed that my husband's sock had a hole in it. I watched him for a while and every time he'd laugh his toe would stick out further. Pretty soon his whole toe was out of the hole and had turned purple, like it was choking to death.

"Honey, why don't you take those socks off? Your toe looks miserable."

He looked down and wiggled it a couple of times. "It's okay," he said. "It just hurts when I walk." He looked at me reproachfully.

"You don't have to wear those socks. You have at least six other pairs in your drawer."

"I know, but I don't like any of them. They're either too thin, or too short, or stiff. I like these socks."

"You've told me that for a year, but I can't find any more exactly like them. Those will have to be thrown away — they're gone."

"Can't they be mended?"

"Are you kidding?"

"No. My mother used to darn our socks."

70

The next day I went to the neighborhood variety store.

"Darning thread?" The high-school clerk looked bewildered. "I'll have to ask my boss." She conferred with a middle-aged lady in a blue smock and then came back to report, "We haven't stocked darning thread for years. But my boss suggested embroidery thread."

That afternoon I laboriously made a crude, basket-weave stitch all over the hole in his sock, and even made a few stitches in the other sock where it was getting thin. I felt proud and homebodyish as I put the pair in his drawer.

The next morning after he had showered and shaved, he came stalking into the kitchen in his shorts looking like he did the night the transmission went out.

"Why did you tie knots in the toes of my socks?" His voice trembled.

"Knots?" I cried. "I *darned* them!"

In reply, he tossed the socks into the wastebasket.

Well, there's no pleasing some people. Anyhow, those socks made the best dustcloths — after I cut out the knots.

———

"For everything there is a season . . . a time to rend, and a time to sew" (Eccl. 3:1,7).

"No one sews a patch of unshrunk cloth on an old garment, for the patch will pull away from the garment, making the tear worse" (Matt. 9:16).

Some things are beyond mending and have to be replaced. And now that we are Christians, maybe some of our non-Christian activities should be replaced.

OLD GRAY HEAD

MY HUSBAND IS GETTING PREMATURELY gray. At least I think it's premature. We're not near old enough for gray hair. So one evening after the kids went to bed I ran my fingers through his hair.

"Honey, why don't you let me do something about your white streak?"

"I like my white streak," he said, moving his head from under my fingers. "Your mother said it made me look distinguished."

"That's the point," I answered. "You're just beginning to get somewhere at the company. You don't want them to think you're too old."

"Too old! It was just a few months ago you made me buy that dark suit so they would think I was older and more responsible."

"True. But some people age quickly. Why don't you just let me put a little of my rinse on it tonight? It'd be fun!"

"Your rinse wouldn't do. My hair is almost black and yours is brown."

"I could make it double strength."

He wasn't in favor of it, but he let me put the stuff on.

"But just on that white streak," he made me promise.

When we were through and he had combed his hair, he looked much younger; but he wasn't convinced. He peered at himself critically.

"Isn't that place a different shade?"

"All the more natural," I said. "Nobody's hair is the exact same shade all over their head."

The next morning, however, in the daylight that white streak was bright orange. I felt a shiver of apprehension as I kissed him good-by.

That night when he came in I hurried to him with his slippers in my hand, but he wasn't glad to see me.

"This has been the most humiliating day of my life," he said. "Everybody, from the mail kid on up to the boss, has stared at me and snickered." He leaned over to untie his shoes and his head in the late afternoon sunshine looked like a Hallowe'en decoration.

"I don't know how you're going to do it, but I want my white streak back."

White shoe polish? Paint? My mind raced around for a solution. *Bleach* solution. That was the answer.

After dinner I scrubbed his head with laundry detergent, and though it was risky I applied a mild solution of bleach to the flame-colored hair. I won't go into the details of his grumbling and threatenings, but finally his streak was back. Not snow white, but at least not red — and just a teency bit wider. When we went to bed he smelled like a laundry bag and acted like an old grouch. Maybe we *are* old enough for gray hair. I certainly feel older, and wise enough not to try that again.

" . . . *you cannot make even one hair white or black"*
(Matt. 5:36).

*"You shall rise up before the hoary [gray] head, and
honor the face of an old man, and you shall fear your
God: I am the LORD"* (Lev. 19:32).

If we have put our hearts in His hands, our age and the
color of our hair is unimportant.

WASHED UP

I PUT A LOAD OF CLOTHES IN THE WASHER and then plugged in the vacuum sweeper. Today I was determined to get the whole house clean and the washing done. As soon as I turned on the vacuum sweeper, I thought I heard ringing, so I ran to the phone; but there was nothing on the other end but the dial tone.

I started the sweeper, and again I thought I heard ringing. This time I went to both doors.

"My imagination," I said aloud and turned on the sweeper. I was almost through vacuuming when I thought I heard water splashing. Of course I didn't turn off the sweeper, because it was obvious there was something about the tone of the motor that made me hear things.

When I saw water rising in the kitchen, though, I knew there was nothing wrong with my hearing. Water was splashing out the top of the washing machine, and the utility porch and most of the kitchen were already under about half an inch of water.

Intelligently, I pulled the sweeper plug out and then stared stupidly at the washing machine. There must be something I could do. At last I had sense enough to pull the plug on the machine, and the water stopped cascading down its sides. It was hot and soapy, and my soaked tennis shoes made belching noises with every step.

When the water reached the dining room, I came to life. I couldn't let it soak the carpet. I ran to the bathroom, gathered an armload of dirty towels from the hamper, and dumped them close to the doorway. They were soaked in ten seconds. I piled all the rest of the dirty clothes around them, trying to form a dike, but the water was determined to get into the dining room. I grabbed clean bath towels out of the linen closet, put them next to the carpet, and then picked up the broom.

After I opened the back door I gave my first big *swoosh* with the broom just as the dog came running up the back steps. He survived that wave, but went coughing and yelping across the backyard. It took the rest of the morning to get the floor mopped up, bail out the washing machine, rinse the clothes in the bathtub, and hang them outside. (The dryer for some reason won't work now either.)

My husband is working on them now. He said something about a cellulose stitch(?) not working, and that possibly we ought to get a new washer-dryer combination! Oh, joy! And you should see my kitchen floor — it's never been so clean.

"Purge me with hyssop, and I shall be clean; wash me, and I shall be whiter than snow" (Ps. 51:7).

" . . . you were washed, you were sanctified, you were justified in the name of the Lord Jesus Christ and by the Spirit of our God" (1 Cor. 6:11).

It's a great feeling to have our clothes washed and our house cleaned up — but the greatest feeling is to have our lives cleaned up by Jesus Christ.

PIANO RECITAL

THERE IS NOTHING THAT CAUSES MORE emotional stress for a mother than her child's first recital.

When my son was only four he picked out on the piano, "My Country 'Tis of Thee," and from that time I knew he was destined to be another Paderewski. Other members of the family were not that certain. In fact, everyone always disappeared between 4:00 and 5:00 in the afternoon when he practiced. His "plink, plink (Wait — I have to start over), plink-plank, clunk, clunk (Oh, oh, have to start over), plink-plank" was pretty wearing, but it was worth it all the night of his recital.

Due to an oversight, his father had scheduled a fishing trip, so my mother went with us that night. The recital was held in the old Community Church. Before the program started, all the pupils raced around, pounded out "Chopsticks" and "Heart and Soul" on the piano, knocked over the flag, and got into the cookies. But at last the teacher, Mrs. Pfleggler, got their attention and had all of them sit in the first two rows. The program began.

About an hour later, my mother said in a stage whisper, "If I'd known it was going to be this long I wouldn't have come." The program *was* a little long. Mrs. Pfleggler shouldn't have had all forty-one students perform in one evening.

As I traced the recital's progress on the program, my hand began to shake. Only three more and then my son! I craned my neck to see how he was. He and another boy were punching each other and making faces. I tried to get his attention, but mother pulled me down and whispered hoarsely, "Sit down! You're causing more disturbance than he is!"

Mrs. Pfleggler had to announce him twice before he heard, then he leaped up on the platform, shirttail out and hair mussed, and took his place at the piano. My heart pounded wildly and my deodorant failed.

With chubby fingers poised masterfully over the keys, he began to play:

"Plink, plink, plank, plank, plunkety, plunk. Plink, plink, plink, plink, plunk, plunk, plunk."

It was over! He had done it perfectly. It seemed to me the applause was deafening until I realized I was the only one clapping.

" . . . a son of Jesse . . . skilful in playing. . . . and the Lord is with him" (1 Sam. 16:18).

"All your sons shall be taught by the Lord, and great shall be the prosperity of your sons" (Isa. 54:13).

We're anxious for our children to learn how to use their talents. Let's be just as eager to teach them about Jesus.

CONTENTED MALCONTENT

EVERY TIME I LOOK AT NEW FURNITURE, I get the "discontents." The room settings in the furniture stores are so gorgeous. When I compare our shabby, old-fashioned living room set I get jealous. But our budget says no new furniture this year.

When I get the "discontents," I usually work them off by moving furniture around. Yesterday was one of those days. I started by dragging and pushing the couch to the opposite wall, which meant I had to take down the pictures and rearrange them. That left the wall full of holes — but I mixed some Will-hold glue with bath powder, and now you can barely see the holes. The wall smells nice, too.

After I moved the couch, I had to vacuum — the couch was outlined on the rug in gray fuzz. I also found a Barbie doll arm and several M & M's, which I resisted eating. I had to move all the other furniture so the room would be balanced; and I vacuumed, polished the furniture, and washed three months' dust off the plants.

I remembered a cute idea I had seen in a magazine, so I moved my husband's chair and end table to form a room divider between the dining room and living room. It looks good, but I'll probably have to put it back where it was. My husband had to work late last night, and when he came in, he didn't turn on the dining room light, and he walked right into it. I understand he practically did a flip. I'm glad I didn't wake up. I hate long drawn-out discussions in the middle of the night.

This morning when I went into the living room, it actually made me gasp — it looked beautiful. Everything is clean and looks different. The way the light hits the furniture now it hardly looks soiled. Maybe we don't need new furniture.

"A sound heart is the life of the flesh, but envy the rottenness of the bones" (Prov. 14:30 KJV).

" . . . for I have learned to be content whatever the circumstances" (Phil. 4:11).

Window shopping isn't the best way to count our blessings.

HELPMATE

MY HUSBAND WANTED ME TO TYPE A business letter for him yesterday. After I had typed the company name and address I said, "Who does it go to? Or, to whom does it go?"

"I don't have a specific name," he said. "Just start out with 'Gentlemen.' "

"I'll bet a woman opens it," I said. "Maybe I'd better put 'Gentlewoman.' "

"That's ridiculous!" he snorted. "Now you've made me forget my first sentence. Just put 'Dear Sir.' "

"Honey" — I shook my head with disgust — "this letter represents *you*. 'Dear Sir' is so antiquated. Nobody uses 'Dear Sir' any more."

"All right!" He jumped up and looked over my shoulder. "What have you got so far?" He read the name and address and said, "If you're sure a woman is going to open it, how about 'Dear Madam' or 'Dear Ms.'?"

I shook my head. "No, because a man might open it. Or a sweet little old lady who would resent being called Ms."

"Well I don't care what you call them!" He was scowling and jiggling the keys in his pocket. "But every letter I get starts out 'Gentlemen'!"

I raised my eyebrows and tipped my head back.

"See? Even if a man opens it, two to one he's *not* gentle."

"Just skip the salutation! Let's get the letter done and we can decide later." He dictated the rest of it and then said, "Why not 'To Whom It May Concern'?"

I compressed my lips and sighed.

"Shows a lack of interest on your part," I said. "If you don't even care who gets your letter" — he made a gasping sound — " 'To Whom It *Will* Concern' would be better." He closed his eyes and leaned against the wall. "Or, how about 'Dear Friend'?"

"How can I call somebody I don't even know 'Dear Friend'?"

"I've got it!" I typed rapidly, *Hello.*

He stared at the word and then let out a little moan.

"Forget the letter." He started toward the door.

"Where are you going?"

"To the phone. I'll call them."

"Live in harmony with one another. . . . Don't be conceited" (Rom. 12:16).

"Now as the church submits to Christ, so also wives should submit to their husbands in everything" (Eph. 5:24).

Some of us may be smarter than our husbands, but the Lord commands us to honor them — and *He* is smarter than we are.

POW-ROW

I WAS TELLING MY SISTER ABOUT A friend who seems to be giving me the cold shoulder.

"I don't understand it," I wailed. "I just don't understand it! I've been so good to her. I typed stencils for her Good News Club. I kept her kids for her. *I mean any time* she wanted to leave those three kids with me I've kept them, morning, noon, or night. When we go on trips I always bring her a souvenir. Like last summer when we went to that beach resort, I brought her a stuffed teddy bear — and it cost quite a bit, too; but she had mentioned one time she thought they were so darling, and I do too, and I knew she'd just flip over this one, and so even though it cost a lot, I went ahead and bought it, just because I want her to know she's thought of and loved. Can you understand why she would avoid me? I mean, now, after we've been friends for two years and are just getting to know one another. Do you have any idea, sis? Because, if I have bad breath or something, please, please tell me, okay? Sis? Hey — you have a faraway look in your eyes — "

"Frankly, I wish I were far away when you get on these talkathons."

"What?"

83

"Well, you said to tell you if you have bad breath or something. You've got T.T.M."

"What do you mean?"

"I mean that sometimes you *talk too much!*"

Silently I vowed I would never utter another word. Aloud I said, "Do you really think that's why she's avoiding me? Are you trying to tell me that she is bored with my conversation? Because if that's so, I want to know it. After all, half the battle is recognizing your problem."

"You've got it."

"What?"

"T.T.M.," she reiterated.

That night I told my husband about our discussion.

"Do you agree with my sister? Now just tell the truth, because I'd like to correct my faults. I don't want people hating me, avoiding me, or talking behind my back, because I commit the social error of trying to be in the limelight. I *despise* being around people who can't ever be quiet. Just answer me straight — do you think I talk too much?"

He sighed wearily and nodded his head.

I went into the bathroom and pasted a Band-Aid on my mouth. I painted a pretty cupid's-bow mouth on it with my lipstick. I didn't want to look ugly, even if I felt that way.

"Your own mouth condemns you, . . . your own lips testify against you" (Job 15:6).

"In all toil there is profit, but mere talk tends only to want" (Prov. 14:23).

Let's ask the Lord to help us not to talk so much, but rather, to be good listeners — especially during prayer.

SLEEPY-TIME GAL

LAST NIGHT, FOR SOME REASON, I couldn't sleep. At first it was too hot and I got up and turned on the fan. It's the noisiest "silent" fan I've ever heard, but its motor throbbed out cool air, which felt wonderful on my damp p.j.'s, and I almost got to sleep. Then my husband began to snore. Compared to him the fan *is* silent. He drew in his breath with a long, snorty gasp and let it out like a balloon turned loose. Over and over and over. I got up and went into the living room and lay down on the couch, which is quite comfortable. But I was tense and alert, like a cat on the prowl. I tried to recite Bible verses and finally dropped off somewhere between "The Lord is my Shepherd" and "All have sinned."

I awoke cold and shivering. I went to the bathroom, read a couple of pages in a book, and then crept back in beside my warm husband and snuggled up. He was still gasping and ballooning, and I couldn't make up my mind if this warm, cuddly feeling was worth all the noise. I realized then that there wasn't going to be any sleep for me and I felt a little frantic. I thought of all the work I had planned for the next day. A big basket of clothes to press and half a bushel of peaches that would spoil pretty soon. I turned onto my stomach. *I had to get some sleep!* I turned on my left side. No wonder people took sleeping pills. "Lord, please make me go to sleep." I flipped over on my right side and my husband stopped snoring — for ten seconds. Thoughts tumbled around in my head like clothes in a dryer. Would we ever get out of debt? Would I remember to make appointments for the kids' teeth to be cleaned? Would Julie and Doug get back together on "Days of Our Lives"?

This is stupid! I thought, and I flounced out of bed and went into the kitchen. I closed the door so the rest of the family wouldn't be disturbed and set up the ironing board. I finished off the basket in less than an hour. As wide awake as a four-year-old at a party, I started on the peaches. In the next hour I got twenty containers in the freezer and I don't know how many bites in me. I washed up all the mess, cleaned off the counters, and even washed some of the cupboard doors. After I mopped the floor, I stepped out back to hang the mop and listened to the three A.M. silence. The dog got up from his bed and wagged his tail feebly. He yawned, and I could see all of his teeth and part of his throat. I yawned, but he wasn't looking at me. I went back to bed and slept.

This morning I feel like a queen! The two things I dreaded are done! What a wonderful way to cope with insomnia. But I hope it doesn't become a habit.

———— ⁊⁊∾⁊⁊ ————

"She rises while it is yet night and provides food for her household . . ." (Prov. 31:15).

Sometimes the Lord allows us to have a wakeful night — not to do housework, perhaps, but to do His work — praying for the saints.

HOME MOVIES

I FEEL A LITTLE VINDICTIVE THIS MORN-
ing. We had a family get-together last night, and our
relatives really hurt my feelings. I may just punish them by
never showing any of my slides or movies again.

I'll admit I'm not the greatest photographer in the world,
and some of the movies that I took out the windshield of
the car make even me a little sick. But couldn't they simply
close their eyes during the worst parts instead of muttering,
"Good grief"? One of the men was actually rude enough
to go outside while I was showing the movie where the
baby and the dog are sleeping together on the rug. Maybe
I shouldn't have shot the whole fifty feet on them, because
sleeping babies and dogs aren't very active. But how
about the reel of the girls playing badminton? There was
plenty of action in that one. Cousin Les pointed out in his
superior way, that I should have focused on the net instead
of the shuttlecock. Pick, pick.

The family was a little more interested when I began to
show slides. There was one tense moment, actually about
fifteen minutes, when I got a slide stuck in the projector.
Everybody had an idea how to get it out, including my

husband who thought I should burn it out. I thought my brothers-in-law were going to have a fight over it, the way they were glaring and mumbling at each other, and shoving that little rod back and forth. They finally got the slide out, but I'll never be able to show it again.

Confidentially, I was a little provoked at myself when I discovered every slide was in sideways in the next carousel. It would have taken too long to turn them, so I suggested that everyone lean forward and turn his head sideways. But they didn't take kindly to this suggestion, and almost in one voice they said it was time to go home. What really hurt my feelings was they didn't wait to see our vacation slides.

Well, maybe I can show them next time. And I'm sure they'll want to see the pictures I took of them last night.

———⁓∾⁓———

"Love . . . does not boast, it is not proud. It is not self-seeking . . ." (1 Cor. 13:4,5).

". . . in humility consider others better than yourselves. Each of you should look not only to your own interests, but also to the interests of others" (Phil. 2:3,4).

If we allow ourselves to be Christ-centered, we won't become self-centered.

PINTO BEANS

IT HAD BEEN A LONG BUT FUN DAY. I had helped the club I belong to with a rummage sale. We had rented an empty store building and arranged all our stuff in it, and then every day for a week members took turns minding the store. I hadn't done anything strenuous that day, but just being there for eight hours was tiring; and since it was for a good cause I was reasonably sure my family wouldn't complain about a meal of leftovers.

I had only been home about fifteen minutes, long enough to peel off my good clothes and put on my old robe so my stomach could relax, when I heard my husband drive in. The car door slammed and then slammed again. I heard voices and ran to the window. Oh, my, no! He had brought some man home with him. I ran to the bedroom, flung my robe into the air, and put my clothes back on. Fortunately I hadn't hung them up.

I was smearing on lipstick when my husband called, "Hey, sweetie — we have a guest."

I didn't trust the tone of my voice, so I didn't answer. That was one thing he promised never to do — bring home unexpected company. I patted a few strands of wild hair back into place and went into the messy living room. Deftly, I kicked a tennis shoe under the couch and prayed that the man was near-sighted.

"Dear, this is Paul MacIntosh, our regional director. I promised him a home-cooked meal."

"Oh?" my stiff lips smiled, but there was hate in the look I gave my husband.

"I tried to call you," he said, and his eyes begged for understanding, "but you weren't home."

"This was the day I helped at the rummage sale," I said, still smiling over gritted teeth. "Maybe we could all go out for dinner." Mr. MacIntosh looked sad.

My husband spoke up, "Mac's been on the road for almost four weeks — "

"I'd give anything just to sit down in a home," Mr. Mac said piteously. "I don't care what we have to eat." I went into the kitchen, making faces all the way.

I fried all the meat I could find — a little dab of hamburger, two hot dogs, and four slices of bacon. I mixed leftover corn, beans, spinach, and peas together and garnished them with three raviolis. Way back in the refrigerator I found a big container of pinto beans that I had cooked about a month ago. In all fairness to the family and to Mr. Mac, after I had heated the beans I tasted them and waited fifteen minutes. Since I didn't die or throw up, I figured they were okay.

When Mr. Mac left that evening he shook my hand warmly.

"I don't see how you fixed such a variety of things on such short notice," he said. "And do you know, pinto beans are my favorite? Never get them at home."

Since my husband is going to get a raise, I could probably demand a dinner out, but we still have some of those pintos to clean up.

"Wives, submit to your husbands as to the Lord" (Eph. 5:22).

"Humble yourselves, therefore, under God's mighty hand, that he may lift you up in due time" (1 Peter 5:6).

As we humble ourselves before the Lord, it becomes easier to submit ourselves to our husbands — and the Lord has promised to *lift us up* in due time!

SKATEBOARD

I WAS ALONE IN THE HOUSE, AND THERE WERE the skateboards, idle in the front hall. I looked out at the sidewalk and recalled how graceful the children looked as they sailed by on their skateboards. It seemed so easy. I put the toe of my shoe on one and moved it back and forth. Should I or should I not? Immediately my two natures began a debate.

"Absolutely not. You're too old."

"I'm not that old."

"You could break your back."

"Just standing on it? Not likely."

"Listen, stupid, those are ball-bearing wheels. Standing on it would be like stepping on spilled oil on a dance floor."

"How about if I hold onto this door-facing? I just want to try it."

"Why take a chance? You're alone in the house. What if you fall and crack your head?"

"I won't fall. I'll be careful."

"Have you already forgotten last spring when you fell off your bike? Your ankle still hurts. You were being careful then."

92

"Yes, but I didn't see that hole until the front wheel —"

"See? Accidents do happen. Forget the skateboards and get your housework done."

I ignored myself and picked up a skateboard. I spun the wheels and they made a soft (sinister?) whirring sound. I put it down on the carpet and pushed it back and forth.

"I don't see how it could be dangerous on the carpet. The wheels hardly roll. After all I *can* skate."

"Is that what you call it? Your neck has hurt ever since you fell at the Sunday school skating party. I'm warning —"

"Look! I'm standing on it! Ta-da!"

"Heaven help us. Some people never learn."

"Look! One leg! Isn't that good?"

"Hope our insurance covers skateboard accidents."

"Don't be such a spook. It's learning things like this that keep us young."

"If it doesn't kill us first."

"Here goes one quick little shove!"

Thank You, Lord, for letting me fall on the sofa.

———⁓♥⁓———

". . . but the LORD was not in the fire; and after the fire a still, small voice" (1 Kings 19:12).

When we are willful, ignoring God's still, small voice, we usually end up being woeful.

93

FULL MOON

THERE WAS A FULL MOON LAST NIGHT, and my husband and I sat on the back steps and looked at it.

"Romantic, huh?"

"Yes. But it doesn't seem as romantic as it used to. Just think, men have actually walked around on it."

"Ridden, too," he added.

"And now they're exploring Mars. It makes me feel so ignorant."

"Why?"

"Because I just don't understand how scientists can figure out all that stuff. When they talk about whether or not there are living organisms on Mars, and if there are, if they're chemical or biological — I just don't understand it."

"It's because you won't read. You could learn."

"Not scientific stuff. My mind just seems to shut off."

"Maybe you don't want to understand anything about outer space."

"Yes, I do. But how can I understand outer space when I don't understand inner space? I still don't understand how

the radio works." My husband shook his head in disgust.
"Something else I don't understand — " I continued.
"The earth revolves around the sun, right?"

"Right."

"And the earth is also spinning all the time?"

"Yep."

"Well, how come our daylight and dark aren't just flipping back and forth like lighted windows on a train?"

He laughed and gave me a little hug.

"You're so funny!"

"Don't laugh at me — I really want to know."

But maybe he was right. Maybe I honestly don't want to know. I'm happy just being an earthling. I don't even enjoy flying. But I know there's no stopping scientific progress. Before long they'll have stations out in space, and then outposts on the moon and Mars, and then cities. . . .

Maybe our own great-grandchildren will sit on their moonstone back steps and look at earth and say,

"Romantic, huh?"

<hr>

"When I look at thy heavens, the work of thy fingers, the moon and the stars . . . what is man that thou art mindful of him?" (Ps. 8:3,4).

It's great if we know planetary science. But it's vital that we know Jesus Christ as Savior.

THE WHOLE TRUTH

MY FRIEND MARY AND I WERE TALKING about the importance of communicating. I said, "In order to have peace and harmony the members of a family have to be open and truthful with one another."

"I know what you mean," she said. "For six years every wash day I had to turn my husband's T-shirts right side out and it made me so irritated! One day I said to him, 'Why are your T-shirts always wrong side out?' and he said, 'I thought you wanted me to turn them.' All those years!" We both laughed.

The next morning I was telling my husband about it, and suddenly he said,

"Please don't scramble my egg this morning."

"How come? You always want your egg scrambled."

"I always *say* I want scrambled eggs," he corrected, "but this morning make it over easy."

"*Okay!*" I looked at him over my shoulder. "I'll soft-boil it if you want."

"On second thought, I don't want an egg. How about some cooked cereal?"

"Cooked cereal! You hate it."

"I never said I hated it."

"Yes, you did. When we were first married."

"I said I hated to have it *every morning*. When I was a kid I used to wish I could have all the eggs I wanted, but we always had hot cereal. I got tired of it, but I still like it."

"And I like cereal. I never cook it because I didn't think you'd eat it."

"And I never asked for it because I figured if you liked it you would have cooked it."

Ah, communication at last.

But the children still have to learn. I made cocoa last night, and I thought at the time that it seemed thicker and tasted a little different. This morning my daughter said,

"Where is that leftover pancake batter I put in the milk container?"

Now it does seem as if she could have told me that yesterday.

". . . that we may lead a quiet and peaceable life in all godliness and honesty" (1 Tim. 2:2 kjv).

How much less complicated our lives would be if we would just tell the truth about everything.

MAKE TIME FOR COFFEE

"I THINK ONE REASON YOU CAN'T GET your work done, honey," my mother said, stirring her coffee, "is because you let your neighbors take too much of your time." She had come to help me get caught up. "Every time I call you, somebody is here for coffee."

"I guess that's true, mother," I said, putting on a fresh pot, "but I want to be a good neighbor. Anyway, I really like Lottie and Dorothy and Virginia. We talk about our kids and husbands and share recipes." She nodded.

"I used to like to visit with my neighbors, too, but we always had some work to do while we talked. Embroidery or knitting or mending."

"We eat," I said. "Donuts, rolls, brownies."

"I can see that." She looked at my waist. "By the way, have you got anything to go with this coffee? I never did like it without a bite of something."

I brought out a chocolate layer cake I had intended to have for dinner. I cut a piece for both of us and sat down. The doorbell rang. It was Lottie wanting her morning coffee. I had just given her a piece of cake when Dorothy and Virginia came in.

"We were having coffee at my house," Virginia explained, "and saw Lottie come over here. Besides, I didn't have anything to eat!"

Mother jumped up and cut cake for them while I poured coffee. We sat around and ate, drank coffee, and talked until almost noon. I enjoyed it, although I kept thinking about the washing, the beds, and the dishes in the sink. Mother enjoyed herself too and told my neighbors about her "babies," my dad, and how to cook black-eyed peas.

After they left she said, "You see, honey, your neighbors can take up all your time if you let them." I didn't say anything, not wanting to be disrespectful. But she was right.

"What can I do?" I finally said. "I don't want to hurt their feelings."

"Well, honey, why not tell them the truth?"

The next morning I got on the phone.

"Lottie, will you call Virginia while I call Dorothy? Tell her to come over — I've got a problem. I'll put on the coffee."

" . . . they get into the habit of being idle and going about from house to house. And not only do they become idlers, but also gossips and busybodies, saying things they ought not to" (1 Tim. 5:13).

There's nothing wrong with sharing coffee with our friends — but if we never get around to sharing Christ, that's a sin.

VAN CAMP-OUT

FOR YEARS MY HUSBAND AND I HAVE wanted a motor home but couldn't afford it. However, we found a secondhand van that seemed to be made for us.

Inside it was like a playhouse. Festive curtains hung at each window above charming little cupboards; there was a refrigerator, stove, and stainless steel sink, and the breakfast nook converted to a bed. It was perfect and we could hardly wait to try it.

Getting packed was no trouble at all. By the time I put in a change of clothes for each of us the compact closet was full. We took paper dishes because regular plates wouldn't fit in the cupboards. We didn't take many groceries either, but we did take staples like salt-and-pepper shakers, coffee, and a few packets of sugar. I was a little disappointed when I realized the refrigerator had to have ice, but even after getting a twenty-five-pound chunk, there was still room for a quart of milk and a pound of weiners.

Oh, the excitement of the open road! Every rattle and rumble brought us closer to blue skies and tall pines. The only one in the family who wasn't happy was our dog. He kept sliding back and forth in the three-by-four-foot space, first bumping his head on the refrigerator and then his rear on the table leg. He was panting so I decided he must be thirsty. What a thrill it was to actually pump water out of our own little faucet while steaming up a mountain pass. But he didn't want a drink. He wanted to throw up. I was glad my little kitchen had a roll of paper towels.

At our campsite it didn't take me long to discover I had to duck when I got out of the van from the side door. Happily I had some make-up that hid the purple bruise on my forehead.

The first night in our van was so romantic. I could look out our little windows and see the great expanse of bright stars on blue velvet. But when I relaxed enough to fall asleep, I fell out of bed. We were parked on a slope, so I solved the problem by tucking the roll of paper towels under the mattress. The second night the bed was level because my husband jacked up the front end. I didn't realize it would make the van so much higher, and when I stepped out the door I somersaulted into a bed of pine needles. In the process I drenched myself with a cup of water, which was fortunate — I could have been carrying a cup of hot coffee.

Camping out, even in a van, isn't as convenient as living at home. I never did get used to cooking while in a kneeling position, or stretching out on the bed to dress, or filling the water tank with a teakettle. But the *rest* was so good for us! Especially the rest we got after we went home.

Jesus said: "Come with me by yourselves to a quiet place and get some rest" (Mark 6:31).

It's good for us to get to have a camp-out — but when we go, let's not leave God out.

101

OUT OF ADJUSTMENT

THE PICTURE ON CHANNEL 2 MADE US feel as though we were suffering from double vision.

"I'm sure it's the aerial," my husband said. He kneeled in front of the set and twisted dials and pushed buttons for a few moments. "Must have gotten out of adjustment after that windstorm." He stood up and dusted his hands. "I think I'll go up on the roof and turn the aerial. Can you call to me if there's any change in the picture?"

"Don't you think we should call the repairman?"

"I'll try this first. Do you see how it looks now with that double line around everything?" I nodded. "When it changes call out to me."

I stationed myself so I could see the set and be close to the open window. As my husband left the room Rich Little was beginning his routine on the "Dinah" show. He was so funny! He was just starting to do Jimmy Stewart when I felt a tap on my shoulder. My husband spoke quietly,

"You were supposed to tell me if it changed, re-member?"

"You mean you've already been up on the roof and adjusted it?" He nodded his head with closed eyes. "Well, it didn't change," I said. "Not one bit."

"It would have been nice if you could have told me. There I was up there, turning it carefully, inch by inch and not a word out of you."

"But you said to tell you if it *changed*."

"All right! Now I'm going back up — just keep talking to me. Say, 'no change, no change — better — worse, etc.' Okay?"

I gave him time to climb the ladder, then I stared at the set and began to chant loudly:

"No change — no change — still the same — no change — no — "

He tapped me on the shoulder again.

"Move over. I haven't gone back up yet." He pulled the set away from the wall and did something at the back. "Thought I'd try something else first." He put the set back. "I'm going up now — be sure and let me know immediately if there's a change in the picture." As soon as his back was turned, I saluted and clicked my heels together. I looked out the window in time to see his legs disappearing over the edge of the roof and began to call out,

"No change — no change — " Suddenly the set crackled and flashed. "Wait! Stop! It's worse! Dinah looks like she's in a madman's laboratory!"

"What did you say?" my husband yelled. I went to the window.

"It's terrible! I think it's going to blow up."

"No, it's not. Just keep watching."

"Now it's better, but it's worse."

"How could it be better but worse?" he shouted from the housetop.

"I mean it's better than it was a minute ago but worse than when you first started."

"How is it now?"

103

"It's better! Stop now before it's worse."

"It's worse?"

"No, no, it's lots better. Stop — oh, no, you've passed . . . it was better, but now — "

With dust all over his good blue shirt, my husband sank into his chair.

"Call the repairman. I can't fix it." As I went to the phone I heard him mumble. "I *could* fix it if I had someone to help." I made the call. I came back and reported:

"The repairman said Channel 2 is having trouble with its transmission."

"Then the LORD *God said, 'It is not good that the man should be alone; I will make him a helper fit for him' "* *(Gen. 2:18).*

"Fear not, for I am with you, be not dismayed, for I am your God; I will strengthen you, I will help you . . ." (Isa. 41:10).

Others fail us, and we fail others; but God never fails.

TEMPORARY YELP!

WE WERE HAVING TROUBLE MAKING ENDS meet, so I decided to apply for a steno position in one of those temporary-help services. I stayed up most of the night before I took the test, brushing up on my shorthand and typing. Although I didn't get to type "Now is the time for all good men to come to the aid of their country," I did pass the test.

I expected to have to wait a few days before being called to a job, but they sent me right out to a big office. There were about a dozen men there, and each one had a stenographer. I was assigned to a small, dark-haired, severe-looking man who kept running his pencil up and down columns of figures and saying, "Hmmm."

My desk was placed about four feet in front of his, and arranged so my back was to him. "Severe" didn't talk to me or give me anything to do the first hour, and after I had counted all the rubber bands and paper clips in the drawer, there was nothing else to do. It was warm in the room, and I hadn't had much sleep the night before. Gradually my desk turned into a big blanket, and I had on my pajamas, and that's the last I remember. Suddenly "Severe" shouted,

"Mrs. Graff!"

I leaped out of bed and stood up straight. Every steno and boss in the room were staring at me, and for a moment I couldn't recall where I was. My mouth felt like I'd had a shot of novacaine on one side.

"Sir?"

"Can you stay awake long enough to take a letter?"

"Oh, yes, sir!" I sat down on my steno chair, picked up my notebook and pen, and spun around to face him. All business now, I tried to scoot my chair up close to his desk, but the wheels wouldn't roll. I pitched forward on my knees, flung my notebook out into space, and grabbed the edge of his desk. Slowly, but with dignity, I pulled myself up and peeked over the edge at him.

"Ready, sir."

The technical letter he gave me was unbelievable. Oh I got it down all right. I just couldn't transcribe it. I kept staring at my notes, and finally about three o'clock Severe said,

"Mrs. Graff, I think perhaps you are not suited for this job."

I think perhaps I am not suited for any job. But that's all right. My husband says I spend too much money anyway.

***

"Obey them not only to win their favor when their eye is on you, but like slaves of Christ, doing the will of God from your heart" (Eph. 6:6).

"All who are under the yoke . . . should consider their masters [bosses] worthy of full respect, so that God's name and our teaching may not be slandered" (1 Tim. 6:1).

Let's be glad if we don't have to work outside our homes; but if we do, let's determine to be the best employee, for Jesus' sake.

PLAN AHEAD

A COUPLE OF WEEKS AGO I WATCHED MY neighbor unload groceries from her car. After she had carried in four big sacks and there were still several in the trunk, I turned off the hose and went over to help her. The first sack I picked up split, and steaks, hamburger, chicken, fish, and a roast spilled out on her driveway.

"Why on earth have you bought so much?"

"I buy enough for the whole week," she explained.

"Why? We only live a few blocks from the market."

"I hate to buy groceries. Besides, you save money if you only shop once a week."

"I know — impulse buying."

"Right. Since I've been buying groceries like this, I know I've saved five dollars a week."

"But how do you know what to buy?"

"You have to plan ahead — make menus."

Planning anything isn't one of my strong qualities, but that afternoon I made myself figure out menus for the coming week. It took over two hours, and almost two hours the next day to buy all the stuff. Then I couldn't find enough space in the cupboards or refrigerator to put it away. But I agreed with my neighbor — it was a good feeling to know I wouldn't have to shop again until next week; and since I wouldn't be tempted to buy impulsively, I too would save money.

Monday night one of the kids was sick so I had to put one pork chop back in the meat compartment. Next night's menu called for meat loaf. As usual, more than half of it was left, and I put it in beside the pork chop. Wednesday night I planned to have a stew, but I had forgotten to buy celery, so I had to go to the store that day. Unfortunately, fresh rabbit was displayed in the meat counter. We love fresh rabbit, so I decided we could have the stew the next day. Naturally I needed different vegetables, and what could be better than fresh asparagus? Also, I couldn't resist buying a chocolate chiffon pie.

The following Saturday I discovered the pork chop and hamburger patties had spoiled. There were so many containers of odds and ends in the refrigerator I knew I would never be able to put in the new groceries I planned to buy. When I counted my grocery allowance I was shocked to learn I didn't have enough to buy all the ingredients for the following week's menus. So I tore them all up. Frankly, I miss going to the store every day.

"Therefore do not worry about tomorrow, for tomorrow will worry about itself. Each day has enough trouble of its own" (Matt. 6:34).

It's good for us to plan ahead, but it's bad for us to worry about the future.

BE MY VALENTINE

I LOOKED AT VALENTINES THE OTHER day and although they are beautiful and have lovely sentiments, they don't quite say what I feel. I love my husband, but frankly to give him a card that says, "You always bring me joy," would be a lie. A pretty, old-fashioned one read, "Husband, what would I do without you to turn to when things go wrong?" Ho, ho. Not long ago I took my aunt, who is eighty-two, on a four-hundred mile trip.

"Honey," I said just before we left, "do you realize that Auntie could get sick on this trip? Even die?" He looked mildly sympathetic, then patted me on the shoulder.

"Well, if that happens, don't call me. Call the Auto Club."

I was tempted to buy a big, gorgeous card that pretty well says what I feel:

> You make me happy darling,
> In so many ways,
> There's no way to thank you
> With any word or phrase.

110

But if I had bought that one, he'd turn it over and say,
"You paid a buck for this?"

There was a cute one that had two squirrels in an embrace with hearts popping out all around their heads:

> Hubby, what I wouldn't give
> To spend each moment, hour and day
> Right beside you, just to live
> And never leave you, nor go away.

You'd have to be squirrely to enjoy that much togetherness.

All the verses seemed too mushy for me. I thought about trying to make up a valentine for him, but how can I put into words how my chest seems to drop into my stomach when I see his car turn into our driveway? Or how cozy it is to sit and watch TV with him? Or times when I say,

"You know that lady at church — " and he says,

"Yeah, the one with — " and I say,

"That's her," and we both know who we're talking about? That kind of thing can't be put in a verse.

I think I'll forget a card. I'll cook some corned beef and cabbage and make him some cornbread. He'll get the message.

─────── ⌒⌒⌒ ───────

"For this reason a man will leave his father and mother and be united to his wife, and the two will become one flesh" (Matt. 19:5).

". . . And our fellowship is with the Father and with his Son, Jesus Christ" (1 John 1:3).

No one on earth is closer to our hearts than our husbands — but fellowship with Jesus Christ is even more intimate.

111

GOOD FOR GRANDMA

EVER SINCE I'VE BEEN MARRIED I'VE been guilty of wanting whatever my sister got, especially appliances. When she got a broiler/oven, I didn't think I could live unless I got one; and when she got a blender I wheedled my husband into buying one for my birthday. What sis gets I want. And all these appliances are great. I don't know how our great-grandmothers got along without them . . . but after last week I'm not sure I get along *with* them.

It all started with the pop-up toaster. I especially like toasted heels, but heels won't pop up. They curl over, burn a little, and get caught in the element. This causes much trouble at our house because my husband is a safety fanatic and bellows "Don't!" when I approach the toaster with a knife. He refuses to believe it's a very simple matter to put the point of the knife in the stuck heel and pull it out. He's made such a fuss about the possibility of shock, I've promised not to use a knife any more to get the heel out. I think it served him right when I burned my finger last week.

That finger hurt a lot while I was washing down the

cupboards and ceiling, but I had to do it after I left the top off the percolator. I think all percolators ought to have their lids fastened on with a hinge.

Of course, you can never tell when a hinge will break, as it did on my waffle iron. When the waffle was done, I couldn't raise the lid, so there was nothing I could do but let the waffle burn. Fortunately, everyone had eaten when this happened except me. Unfortunately, I was the only one who wanted waffles in the first place.

Possibly the most disconcerting thing this week was the blender blunder. It was a couple of hours until dinner and I was starving, so I decided to whip up a "diet malt." I put a third of a cup of dry milk in the pitcher, a spoonful of sweetener, five or six ice cubes, and a can of diet pop. Just as I started to lift the pitcher to put it on the blender motor, I noticed the blades, rubber washer, and lock ring away over on the other counter. As I cleaned up the mess, I wondered why I ever thought I had to have a blender. Our great-grandmothers, without benefit of electric appliances, probably got along very well.

"Let your conversation be without covetousness; and be content with such things as ye have . . ." (Heb. 13:5 KJV).

When others seem to have *everything,* it's hard not to be envious, but the Lord knows that what we want may not be what we need.

SCENE OF THE ACCIDENT

AT DUSK ONE EVENING WE HEARD THE terrifying crunch of steel against steel. There was a wreck at our corner! I felt a thrill of excitement as I ran to the scene. There were already some thirty people standing there, grouped around the cars, silent and wide-eyed. One of the drivers got out of his car, limped across the street, and sat down on the curb.

People began to whisper, "What happened?" and others answered, "That car took the right of way and —"

The other driver got out of his car and went over to the first driver. It was so exciting! What would they say to each other? Would there be a fight? I *had* to know. I stepped off the curb and started to tiptoe across a puddle of water coming from one of the cars. About halfway across, my feet suddenly went out from under me and I came down hard, flat on my back. I tried to turn over so I could stand up, but my hands, legs, and feet kept slipping. The puddle wasn't water. It was crankcase oil.

On my stomach I carefully drew up one knee and then the other so I could crawl out of the oil, but my legs flopped straight out. I kept wriggling like a fish in shallow water.

Everyone was staring at me, but no one offered to help pull me out.

Gradually I slithered to dry pavement and got to a standing position. Oil was on the bottoms of my shoes, so when I walked I felt like I was on ice skates. I slipped and slid all the way home, dripping black oil from my blue dress, like some monster from the swamp.

I don't know how many times I shampooed and rinsed my hair before it squeaked, or how many times I lathered my body before I got all the oil off. Even now, especially if it's hot, I smell like a garage.

If there's ever another wreck in our neighborhood I may look at it through the window, but you can be sure I won't be at the scene of the accident.

" . . . he who is glad at calamity will not go unpunished"
(Prov. 17:5).

Why are we glad when we hear of the misfortune of others? God help us to be merciful.

I KNOW I KNOW

WHILE SORTING LAST YEAR'S CHRISTMAS cards I found four from people I didn't know. I took them into the family room and stood in front of the TV.

"Anyone know who 'Terry, Jim, and Family' are?" Nobody did.

"How about 'Carnegie, Betty, Mavis, and Kip'?" Head shaking all around.

"Bert and Thelma?"

"Bert and Thelma who?" my son asked.

"There aren't any last names. Do you know a 'Bert and Thelma'?"

"No."

"Well, then, don't interrupt. Honey," I said to my husband, "here's one maybe you know. 'George, Charlene, and houseapes,' "

"Houseapes? Let me see that." I handed him the card.

"They're probably someone you know at work," I said. He examined the card and handed it back.

"Never heard of 'em."

"Well, who are these people? I have to know."

"Why?" He grinned at me. "If you don't know who

they are, you won't have to send them a card this year."

"You can't do that. I have to send them a card. They must be people in your office." His smile faded.

"I *know* who I know," he said. "Why didn't you find out who they were last year?"

"I'm always too busy at Christmas. Anyway, I'm sure I figured they were *your* friends."

"They're probably *your* friends at P.T.A. or church."

"They are *not*. And I also know who I know!"

I lay awake half the night trying to place those people. They had to be my husband's acquaintances. The next morning I gave him the list of names.

"Honey," I said gently, "it's just possible that even you could have forgotten some of your fellow employee's names. Please check it out, and get their last names and addresses so I can send them a card." As he laid rubber all the way to the corner, I felt smugly confident that by evening he and I both would know who those fellow employees were.

About ten o'clock in the morning however, I had a fearful recollection. Terry, Betty, Thelma, and Charlene were women I had known in my oil painting class last year.

"In the mouth of the foolish is a rod of pride . . ." (Prov. 14:3 KJV).

"I say to every one of you: Do not think of yourself more highly than you ought . . . " (Rom. 12:3).

It hurts our pride to be wrong. But the Lord can give us the strength to admit it.

117

CHEER FOR THE SICK

I ALMOST DECIDED NOT TO VISIT MRS. Morgan in the hospital after the flowers fell off the top of the car, but she is a widow, and it had been three days since her operation. I was sure she needed to be cheered up. I felt pretty upset about the flowers. In the first place, they were out of our garden — several beautiful roses and white asters. I had arranged them in one of my favorite vases, and though I shouldn't brag, it was a lovely arrangement. When I started to leave home, I put the flowers on top of the car while I put some magazines in the front seat. I don't know how I could have been that absent-minded, but I got in and drove away. The vase skidded across the top and smashed to the street when I turned the corner. I thought about stopping to pick up the flowers, but I was late; and besides I didn't want any of the neighbors to know I was that stupid.

At the hospital I paid quite a bit for a tacky little bouquet of daisies, but felt it was worth it if I could be of some cheer. Mrs. Morgan was really glad to see me. She held out her hand, and I kissed her pale little cheek and then sat down on the bed. Hospital beds are high and I had to give a little jump to get up on it. For some reason she gave a yelp. Older people are more nervous, I guess.

"How are you feeling?" I asked. She gave a little gasp, then said,

"Not too well, at the moment."

"I'm so sorry. You had your gall bladder removed, didn't you?" She nodded. I said, "My father had his gall bladder removed a few years ago." There was a spark of interest in her eyes.

"How did he get along?"

I looked down at the tile floor. Now I'd done it.

"He died," I admitted. Better change the subject, I decided, when her chin began to quiver.

"Let me plump your pillow, Mrs. Morgan." I jumped down from the bed. She gave another yelp and, if possible, turned even whiter. Poor little thing. She was so nervous. I fluffed up her pillow, but when I stepped back my elbow knocked over the daisies. She looked so pitiful lying there, wet, with daisies on her chest.

They were changing her sheets when I waved good-by, and she didn't look good at all. I'm so glad I took the time to cheer her up.

" . . . I was sick and you visited me . . ." (Matt. 25:36 RSV).

"Praise be to God . . . who comforts us in all our troubles, so that we can comfort those in any trouble . . ." (2 Cor. 1:3,4).

Calling on the sick takes time — but we can find the time, especially if we remember Jesus said, " . . . you did it for me."

HAPPY BIRTHDAY

DURING JOANIE'S SEVENTH BIRTHDAY party I wondered who said, "Sugar and spice and everything nice — that's what little girls are made of." Maybe the seven little girls wouldn't have been so wild if I had been ready for them. I got the cake baked early that morning and had intended to get a couple of games lined up, but when the mail came, there was the magazine that had the conclusion of "Stiletto to the Stomach," and I was just too weak-willed to resist reading it. When I put the magazine down it was eleven-thirty, and no games planned.

At lunch I said, "Do either of you kids have any ideas about games to play at the party?"

"How about Ship and Shore?" Ronnie asked. "See, you have this rope and one team is the ship, and the other is the shore and you pull — "

"In the house?"

"No, outside. It really goofs up your clothes."

"Oh, *yeah!*" Joanie yelled. "Let's play that."

But when the little girls arrived in beautiful long dresses, hair piled high with sweet curls around shining faces, I knew their mothers would never speak to me again if we played a modern version of tug-o-war.

"What would you girls like to play?" I asked.

Theresa, dark eyes huge behind petite glasses, spoke with wonder and derision:

"Don't you have the games planned?"

Angelica, a child you wanted to hug on sight, leaned on me and whispered,

"I would like to play 'pin the dart on the horse's bottom.' "

I remembered I had several large sheets of construction paper left over from some project, if I could only find them.

"Come, girls, sit at this table," I spoke with authority. "I will soon bring materials for you to create something beautiful."

While I looked under the bed and in the closets I could hear Ronnie heckling the girls:

"Eee-yew! How sick — a *girls'* party!" Much screaming, thumping, a small crash.

"Sick! Sick!" he yelled, as he ran from room to room with all the girls in pursuit. Slam! His bedroom door shut.

I found the crumpled construction paper and got the girls back to the table.

"Now, girls, here is paper in all colors, crayons, glue, and scissors. How would you like to make some lovely placemats?" No one said, "Goodie."

"Let me rephrase that: We are now going to make placemats."

At last it was time to open presents. All the little girls pressed together in a space about four feet square. They reminded me of my chickens at feeding time, as they grabbed at the gifts, pushed in front of one another and bickered. Joanie yanked the paper and ribbons from each gift, barely glancing at its contents before reaching out for the next one.

121

As the girls stood around the cake with lighted candles, singing, there seemed to be a heavenly aura about them. Maybe they *are* made of sugar and spice, but not everything nice.

"[Jesus] said to them, 'Let the little children come to me, and do not hinder them, for the kingdom of God belongs to such as these" (Mark 10:14).

We should try to provide opportunities for our children to learn social graces; and we *must* provide opportunity for them to learn the grace of God.

DREADFUL DRAWERS

LAST WEEK MY MOTHER CAME OVER FOR lunch, and while she was here she discovered a hangnail.

"Where are your nail clippers?" she asked, getting up from her chair.

"I'll get them!" I jumped up and started for the bedroom.

"You don't have to wait on me."

"I know right where they are," I lied. They were either in my make-up drawer or in the middle drawer. Or possibly in my overnight case. I hoped. But wherever they were, I couldn't let her see the mess my drawers were in.

I jerked open the make-up drawer and pawed crazily through the mess. Oh, why, I moaned, do I have seven kinds of eyeshadow when I never wear any? And why had I put a clothespin and a screwdriver in with my make-up? There was lipstick and nail polish, hairbrush, rouge, and glue, but no clippers. *Glue?* No wonder the kids couldn't find it.

The middle drawer was even worse. The last time I had gotten organized, I had put all my jewelry in little boxes on the right side, gloves and scarves in the center, and pantyhose and girdles on the left. Now it looked like a hamper full of clothes had been dumped on a jewelry counter.

"Oh, you slob!" I moaned to myself.

I yanked everything out of the drawer and shook it. I found a pair of scissors that had been lost for months, but no clippers. I rushed to the closet, but they weren't in the overnight case either.

"Never mind, honey," my mother called.

"Somebody must have misplaced them," I answered. But I knew I wasn't fooling her. Humiliated, I handed her the scissors I'd just found.

"A place for everything and everything in its place," she quoted.

After she went home, I looked everywhere for those clippers, including the drawers in the kitchen. Every drawer was a mess, and I hated myself for being so sloppy. I resolved right then to clean every drawer in the house. I started by dumping all the stuff in the kitchen drawers out on the living room carpet. I would have a place for everything and everything in its place. But my husband came home early.

"I thought I'd take you out to dinner," he said, "but since you're in a project — "

"It can wait," I said, scooping the stuff back into drawers.

After dinner I asked my husband to stop at the drugstore.

"How come?" he asked.

"I need a pair of nail clippers."

━━━━━━━━⌘━━━━━━━━

"... train the younger women ... to be self-controlled and pure, to be busy at home ... so that no one will

124

malign the word of God" (Titus 2:4,5).

Housekeeping is a never-ending job, but our neighbors *and* husbands might believe what we say about Christ if they see what we do with our homes.

RUINED ROMANCE

IF THERE'S ANY ROMANCE LEFT IN OUR marriage after today it won't be because of me. Right after my husband went to work this morning, I read an article about keeping romance alive in marriage. The author claimed that most "blah" marriages are due to a "blah" attitude in the wife.

"After marriage, and especially after children," the article said, "women tend to become negligent and lukewarm toward their mate. They forget how important he was to them before marriage, how they lived for the moment they could be together. As a consequence, some men look elsewhere for attention. A wife should be ready to drop what she's doing to be at his side any time he wants her." I felt a stab of guilt. Just last week he had asked me to go with him to get gas in the car and I had refused!

"Before you were married, did you let your husband see you in a ragged bathrobe? Of course not." I looked down at my old tiger robe. It looked like it had the mange.

"Never allow your husband to catch you shaving your legs." That really shook me. I not only had shaved my legs in front of him, but had used his razor.

"Never, never, never let your husband see you in curlers, tweezing your eyebrows, using a depilatory or a facial mask. Don't turn him off with any of these gross grooming chores. Don't let him in on your beauty secrets. The most charming women have an air of mystery about them."

Convinced that I had probably ruined our marriage, I decided *today* I would put romance back into our relationship, and the best place to start was with my hair.

After an hour I finally got the last permanent curler rolled up and sloshed on the remaining solution, which ran down my neck, into my bra and panties. The directions said to wait fifteen minutes. I spread an even coating of pink depilatory paste on the fuzz on my upper lip. It was supposed to stay on seven minutes. That would give me just enough time to lather up my legs and use my own double-edge razor. I was going to be an attentive, lovely woman of mystery.

"Man, this place smells terrible!" My husband was standing in the doorway. "What is that horrible smell?" I dropped the razor and flung my arm across my mouth.

"Home permanent," I mumbled. Why hadn't I heard him come in?

"What's wrong with your mouth? Why do you have soap all over your legs? Good night! It stinks in here!" He backed out of the bathroom and called from the living room:

"I have to drive up the coast to see a customer. Wanted you to come along." Of course I couldn't go.

So, I'm sure I've killed the last trace of romance. I've done all the things the article said not to. But there *is* a glimmer of hope — I might seem mysterious tonight. In fact, he may not recognize me. My hair looks like a red Afro wig, and there's an ugly abrasion on my upper lip.

> *"So, because you are lukewarm — neither hot nor cold — I am about to spit you out of my mouth" (Rev. 3:16).*

Sometimes, without realizing it, we allow our relationships to get lukewarm — not only with our husbands, but also with the Lord.

SELF-SERVICE

"ONE WAY WE COULD SAVE A LITTLE money," my husband said, "would be if you would get your gas at a self-service."

"You're right — but I don't know how to work the pumps."

"They're very simple to operate. Fred says his wife does it all the time."

"She's more mechanically minded than I am. I'd be so embarrassed if I couldn't do it."

"Honey, really, there's nothing to it. They'd show you how."

So, the next time the gas tank was empty, I drove over to the self-service station. There was a big difference in the price of gas, but the thought of trying to work the pump made my heart pound. I forced myself to drive in and pull up by a pump that said "Regular." I timidly opened the car door and started to get out, when a thin, bored-looking fellow with long, stringy hair sauntered over to me.

"How many?" Hope leaped up in me. Maybe he was going to wait on me. I pulled my legs back in and looked up at him.

129

"Do you do the self-service?"

"Nope." He pointed a grimy finger. "You want self-serve, you go over to those pumps."

"Oh. Uh, I've never done it. Would you show me how?"

He rolled his eyes and sighed wearily.

"Okay."

I started the engine and put it in reverse. There was a grinding, clanging sound. I slammed on the brakes and looked out. How that big metal sign got that close to my car I'll never know.

"Wow," I moaned. "I'm so sorry. Guess I'll have to pay for it, huh?"

He shrugged. "It's nothing to me. The boss gets those signs free. I think."

At the pump he said,

"Alls you have to do is, first: flip the numbers over." He turned something so that "Gallons" and "Amount" read "000." He moved back and removed the gas cap. I watched carefully as he picked up the nozzle and put it in the hole. It was simple. I was sure I could do that.

"How much?"

"Fill it up, please," I said.

"It'll take awhile," he said as another car drove in. "It shuts off automatic." He drifted over to the other car. I looked around and noticed a sign: All Sales Cash. No Checks. No Credit Cards. I yanked open my billfold, and all I had was a five dollar bill. The figures on the pump were tumbling: $4.56, $4.57, $4.58 — I ran to the back of the car and yanked the nozzle out and gas poured all over the trunk and some on my foot. I rammed it back in and yelled for him to come and stop it. He got there just as the figures read $5.00.

"Dames," he grumbled as I drove away.

"You get gas?" my husband asked that night.

"Yes."

"Self-service?"

"Yes."

"How was it?"

"Nothing to it." I looked into his eyes. "Well — for some people."

"The LORD preserves the simple; when I was brought low, he saved me" (Ps. 116:6).

We needn't feel bad about the things we can't do. We should feel bad about the things we won't do.

WONDER WOMAN

MY BEST FRIEND CAN DO *ANYTHING*. The last time I went to her house for lunch, I felt so dazzled and jealous I almost ran away. First of all, she is an immaculate housekeeper. She even keeps her fireplace waxed on the inside. She is so neat that the medicine in her bathroom cabinet is arranged alphabetically.

She knows all about interior decorating too. Her drapes hang perfectly (she made them), her picture arrangements are stunning, and her furniture is tastefully arranged. She is so talented she could probably earn a living with her oil painting — she does portraits *and* landscapes — or her decoupage, or her sewing. She not only makes her own and her children's clothes, but she makes her husband's *suits*.

After I've been with her awhile I get numb. I can't take it all in. How does she do it?

Out in her yard she is still a wonder. They have a pool, and who laid the bricks for the planters? You guessed it. Her patio (where there is never a dog bone, tennis shoe, or any out-dated magazines) is cool with the shade of at least one hundred thriving plants.

You might think she would be big, muscular, and ugly;

132

but no, she wears a size ten and looks like a model. She is an excellent cook. Her chocolate pies are two inches high, and her homemade yeast rolls are light and browned to perfection.

Perhaps, you might ask, she is disagreeable, or unkind? No, unfortunately. She is sweet, kind, and fun to be with. She teaches Sunday school and finds time to take her pupils on outings. I know there's no such thing as sinless perfection, but she seems to be flawless.

When I left her house, after a luncheon of shrimp Newburg, I felt like a malformed moron. I was so rattled I tried to get into someone else's Ford. Driving home I thought about what a failure I was compared to her. Hadn't I just that week left a Kleenex in the pocket of my jeans while I washed them? With a lump in my throat I recalled chopping up my plastic straw in the blender, getting a potholder on fire, and trying to brush my teeth with Desitin.

That night my son said,

"If you could trade places with anybody in the world, who would you rather be?"

I looked at him; I thought about his sister and their father, and Tummy and the cats.

I couldn't think of a single person I'd rather be, not even my wonder girl friend.

" . . . envy slayeth the silly one" (Job 5:2 KJV).

"For he knows our frame; he remembers that we are dust" (Ps. 103:14).

We must not be overwhelmed by our limitations. God made us and He loves us, and there is no one we'd trade places with.

133

SIESTA!

AN ARTICLE I READ THE OTHER DAY stated that nothing is as beneficial to the human body as a nap. A little sleep in the middle of the day is supposed to make you look better, be sharper mentally, and be a nicer person to live with. Executives were urged to stretch out in their offices after lunch, on the floor if they didn't have a couch. Employees should put their heads down on their desks at lunchtime and sleep a few minutes; and housewives *must* rest, no matter how busy they are, in order to cope from early morning until late at night.

"Super," I thought, because I really like to take naps, but I always had a guilt complex about them. Now I realized it was my duty to take care of myself. I yawned happily and lay down on the couch right after lunch.

When the phone rang I couldn't remember where I was; I jumped up, ran into the wall, and put the wrong end of the phone to my ear. From a distance I could hear my mother saying, "Hello? Hello?" Before I could turn the phone around, she had hung up. I stumbled back to the couch and thought I would have to tell her about my nap time. She ought to be asleep too.

134

I had just gone back to sleep when the couch began to tremble. There was an ominous rumbling in the distance. I rolled off the couch and staggered toward a doorway. The long-predicted earthquake was happening! But it wasn't an earthquake. They were grading the street. I watched the big yellow machine grumble by and then looked at the clock. I'd been trying to nap for twenty-two minutes.

I was wide awake. Maybe I didn't need a nap; still, that article said. . . . I fell down on the couch and was just getting that delicious stupid feeling when the doorbell rang.

"Would you be interested in a demonstration that is guaranteed to give you more leisure?" said a bright-eyed, intense student. Didn't he know he should be asleep? I shook my head and slammed the door.

I don't think a little sleep in the middle of the day is especially beneficial to me.

———— ❧ ————

" . . . understanding the present time. The hour has come for you to wake up from your slumber, because our salvation is nearer now than when we first believed" (Rom. 13:11).

A nap is all right; but let's not be caught sleeping when we should be awaking others with the gospel of Christ.

REMEMBER?

MY FAMILY HAS BEEN AFTER ME FOR years to either take a memory course or vitamins — something to keep me from being so absent-minded. After last night I decided they were right.

We have dear friends who are almost like family. They live across town, and once or twice a year we all get together for a dinner party. We had planned a Christmas party back in October and all of us women were going to wear long dresses and bring our most exotic dishes. After dinner we would play Bingo and have a gift exchange.

My husband and I were looking forward to it. I got my hair fixed in a beauty shop, and he even got a new suit for the occasion. Yesterday I made my fanciest gelatin salad, a vegetable casserole, and veal scallopini.

That night there was no place to park close to our friends' house, and we had to walk almost a block, me flopping along in my long dress in the dark, both of us loaded down with food and gifts.

When we got to their house, I figured we must be the first ones there because she didn't have the porch light on. After my husband rang the bell, there was a long moment before Phyllis came to the door. She had on her everyday slacks and a blouse. She stared at us as though we were strangers.

"Are we early?" I asked. My wrists were aching from the load. Phyllis opened her mouth.

"Tonight?" she bellowed.

"Quit kidding, Phyllis. This stuff is heavy."

She tried to smile as she opened the screen door.

"Honey," she said, "it's *tomorrow* night! Remember?"

Remember! That awful word. How could I have gotten so mixed up?

Well, it could have been worse. I left all the food and gifts at her house, and after my husband got through saying several unkind things about my brain, he took me out to dinner, and we get to go back to our friend's tonight.

But I think I will try to find out something about a memory course. If I can remember to check into it.

"The memory of the just is blessed . . ." (Prov. 10:7 KJV).

Sometimes the things we blame on poor memory are actually a case of poor organization.

UNCOORDINATED

THERE WAS AN ITEM IN THE PAPER THE other day which stated tennis is *the* game this year. People are spending thousands of dollars on rackets, balls, clothes, and courts. I would like to buy myself a racket, but nobody in my family will play with me. I used to own one, but I gave it to a neighbor kid one summer day after my husband told me, "I'm sorry, honey, but it's just no fun to play with someone who is no competition. This was our fourth 50-love game."

Sports have never been my strong suit. One of my first recollections was trying to get past the second square in hopscotch. When I was nine, the boy next door invited me to play catch with him, but the only way I could catch the ball was for us to stand six feet apart. Later, when all of us kids would play softball, I could never catch a fly or hit the ball hard enough to get on first.

In junior high my lack of ability in sports seemed to get worse. In soccer I kicked my own ankle so much I got a callous on it; in volleyball I got my fist caught in the net; and in square dancing I always returned to the wrong partner.

I was excited when we got to take swimming; but when

all my friends had mastered the diving board, I was still leaning over the edge of the pool, arms over my ears, trying to hold my breath and keep my feet together as I belly-flopped into the water.

In gymnastics I could never keep my knees straight while turning cartwheels; and although I finally learned to do a back bend, I could never spring back up. The teacher finally forbid any more forward flips after I landed flat on my back twice in a row and started to turn blue.

In high school during a physical fitness test, we were supposed to be able to do at least four push-ups, but I couldn't do one. I had to do all the pushing with my stomach.

When we were first married, all our friends were crazy about bowling. My husband's average was 178, mine was 53. I guttered and lofted so many balls the manager of the bowling alley suggested that billiards might be better for me. So I tried that, but the only ball I could get in the pocket was the white one.

There are two things I do pretty well. I can still beat my daughter playing jacks, and I can stand on my head any time, any place. That must take some coordination. Maybe the next time I go shopping I'll at least take a look at tennis rackets.

"Do you not know that your body is a temple of the Holy Spirit, who is in you, whom you have received from God? You are not your own" (1 Cor. 6:19).

" . . . we eagerly await a Savior . . . the Lord Jesus Christ, who . . . will transform our lowly bodies so that they will be like his glorious body" (Phil. 3:20,21).

139

When we're disappointed with our bodies let's remember these comforting facts: (1) the Holy Spirit lives in us right now; and (2) someday we'll have bodies like Christ.

ST. LOUIS BLUES

I DON'T THINK WE'LL TAKE A TRIP THIS year on our vacation. My husband says gas is too high, but I think the real reason is that he doesn't want to get lost again. I've always been the navigator on our trips, and I thought I was a good map reader, but I may have lost my skill. It's not all my fault, though. I think there's a sadistic agreement between the map companies and the sign makers never to agree on the number and name of a highway.

For instance, last year when we left Louisville, Kentucky, the map showed that we were to take highway #150 to St. Louis.

"Keep watching for #150 and the words *St. Louis,*" my husband warned.

"That's simple," I smiled. "You worry too much."

"Really?" He started the car. "How about Phoenix? I thought we were on our way to Flagstaff and we ended up in Globe."

"Yes, but that wasn't my fault, remember? The map—"

" — and Albuquerque? I had always wanted to go to Santa Fe, and where did you lead us?"

"Tucumcari," I mumbled. I got a good grip on the road map. I wouldn't get us lost this time.

As we came to the outskirts of Louisville, we had to make a choice. We either had to take #65 or #264. (Not a sign about highway #150 or St. Louis.)

We agreed we'd better stop at a service station and ask.

"Take #65 right on through town to #460, then git yourself on to #150. You cain't miss it."

"Did you get that?" my husband barked as we got back on the highway.

"Of course," I said calmly, but my finger shook a little as I tried to find the numbers the man had mentioned.

Suddenly we were swept along in heavy traffic. Green and white overhead signs flipped by in rapid succession: EASTERN PARKWAY, WEST; NORTH TURNPIKE, RIGHT; INDIANAPOLIS 65, 62, 60; JEFFERSONVILLE, CINCINNATI 42 AND 60." But where, oh, where was #150 or ST. LOUIS?

"Which way?" my husband kept shouting. His knuckles were white on the steering wheel, and he was hunched forward like a jockey on a horse.

At last we were through town and on our way to — Columbus?

We finally got to St. Louis, and the dirt road we had to take to get to #150 was forty-eight miles of the prettiest scenery in Indiana.

❧

". . . wide is the gate, and broad is the road that leads to destruction . . . narrow the road that leads to life . . ." (Matt. 7:13, 14).

There may be many ways to a destination here on earth, but there's only one way to heaven: believe on the Lord Jesus Christ.

FRIENDSHIP

"MOMMY," MY DAUGHTER CALLED, "TEACHER is sick and all of us kids are supposed to send her a get-well card. Will you take me to the store to buy one?"

"Let's look at the ones we have on hand," I suggested.

"Oh, not those crummy old things!" she whined. "I want to send her a pretty card."

"Let's look," I insisted as I struggled to get a drawer open in the desk. It was jammed full of cards and stationery that no one in the family will use.

"They're all ugly," she declared. "Why do we have this kind?"

"You know why. One of the ladies in W.M.C. was selling stationery, and I wanted to help her out," I said. Did I really want to help her or was I just too chicken to say no? "How about this one?"

"I don't want to send her a dopey-looking dog with his head bandaged: 'Here's hoping you'll soon be *pup* and around.' " She made a face. "How sick!"

"Hey, mom," my son called from the kitchen. "I can't find any room in the fridge to put these cans of pop."

"Move something around."

"Why do you keep all these bottles of vitamins in here?"

"They're not vitamins," I shouted. "They're food supplements."

"Who takes them?"

"Nobody!"

"But there's nine bottles of 'em. How come — "

"Never mind!" I yelled. I didn't want to admit it was another example of my cowardly generosity. My husband won't touch those supplements. I've tried to eat them, and I'm sure they're the reason I put on four pounds in a week. The friend who sold them to me claimed they had no caloric value, but I ate so much other food trying to get the taste of them out of my mouth, I gained.

Leaning over my daughter's shoulder, I asked, "Found a card you can use?"

"Do I have to use one of these?" She looked up at me and sniffed. "You smell different."

"Do you like it? It's some of the new cologne I bought from Marilyn. Since we're neighbors, I thought I ought to buy it."

"It smells kind of like bacon."

There ought to be a law to keep friends from trying to sell you stuff. But I'm glad there's not. Then I couldn't invite any of my friends to my Tupperware parties.

"A man that hath friends must show himself friendly" *(Prov. 18:24).*

"No one has greater love than the one who lays down his life for his friends. You are my friends if you do what I command" *(John 15:13,14).*

To be a friend costs time, effort, and sometimes money — but Jesus gave His life to become our *best* Friend.

PARALLEL PARKING

WHEN I TOOK MY DRIVER'S TEST SEVERAL years ago, I had a kind, fatherly type examiner who made allowances for my poor driving.

"I know you're scared," he told me.

When I had to parallel park, he chose a place where I could simply glide into it, or else I'm sure I'd never have passed the test.

All these years I have avoided parallel parking. If a shopping center doesn't have diagonal parking, I don't care what they have on sale, I won't go.

Recently I had to visit a neighboring town on business for my husband. The night before, I said to him,

"I just know I'll have to park at the curb. That little town doesn't have any parking lots." He went over to the desk and took out three dominoes.

"Say there's a car here and here," he said, and he placed two dominoes lengthways, with a space between them. He looked to see if I was paying attention. "This is you." He put his fingers on another domino. "You pull up alongside the first car, cramp your wheels to the right as hard as you can, and then back up gently. When your back

145

wheels get here" — he moved the domino — "then stop and swing the wheel to the left. Then ease in. You'll be right against the curb."

When I left the next morning I was worried, but I felt pretty sure I could park if I had to. Maybe there would be a big space in front of the place, or if I had to walk two or three blocks, so what? But it was just as I feared — bumper-to-bumper parking all through the main section of town. I found a parking spot about a block from the place I was supposed to go. It was in front of the town's pool hall. I took a deep breath, tried to remember Operation Domino, and idled up alongside the first car. A couple of teenage boys came out of the pool hall and leaned against the building. They stared at me with just a hint of a smile on their lips. I could feel sweat pop out on my forehead. I cramped the wheels to the left and eased back. Suddenly both fellows looked horrified and yelled,

"*Hold it!*" Oh, yes. I remembered. To the *right* first. I straightened the wheels, pulled up, and tried again. The fellows were at the curb now, making motions and measurements and shouting warnings and encouragement. Just as I began to roll neatly into the space, I felt a hard jolt.

"*Hold it!*" they yelled again (too late). "Now you've locked bumpers."

One of the fellows got up on the bumpers and began to jump up and down. Out of the corner of my eye I saw a crowd gathering. One old man with a pot belly sauntered out to the middle of the street for a better view.

On the next try my back wheel hit the curb so hard it jerked my neck. On the next try I rammed the car behind. On the next try, through tears, I could see that I had finally gotten into the space, but was still two feet from the curb. Everywhere I looked men were staring at me, shaking their heads or smiling.

146

Suddenly I yanked it into "drive," cramped the wheels as hard as I could, and shot out of that space. Pot-belly leaped back, and I laid rubber for a block.

I still haven't taken care of that business, and I'm too ashamed to go back. But I'm going to have to do it, so I guess I'll work out with the dominoes tonight.

"Endure hardship with us like a good soldier of Christ Jesus" (2 Tim. 2:3).

"Have not I commanded you? Be strong and of good courage; be not frightened, neither be dismayed; for the LORD your God is with you wherever you go" (Josh. 1:9).

When we run away from our problems, we usually have to go back; so it's better to face them, knowing the Lord our God is with us.

MY NOSE KNOWS

I HAVE A BIG NOSE. NOT PHYSICALLY — my outside nose is short; but my inner nose, the "smeller," is huge and hyperactive. I lay awake most of one night last week smelling and resmelling the spaghetti and meatballs we'd had for dinner. I stuck my nose in the pillow, but I couldn't stand the smell of the foam rubber. I can smell a sliver of onion three rooms away, and I can usually tell where the kids have been by the way they smell: sweet and greasy — donut shop; cigar smoke — bowling alley; sweaty and dusty — baseball game.

When we go any place in the car, I usually smell something burning and begin to worry.

"Honey, did you check the water?" I ask. "The engine smells hot."

"The water's fine. Everything's okay."

"But I tell you, I smell something. Maybe the transmission — "

So far there's never been anything wrong with the car when my husband grits his teeth and skids into a service station on two wheels. But I can't help it if I worry, and it's better to be safe than stranded somewhere.

Last night I turned up the furnace thermostat, and it wasn't long until I could smell rubber burning. I sniffed loudly a couple of times, but my husband ignored me. I hated to bother him because he was tired and had just sat down to watch the news, but I was sure there was something on fire.

"Honey, I hate to disturb you, but I think we're having furnace problems. Do you smell rubber burning?"

"No, I do not smell rubber burning, and if there was furnace trouble it wouldn't smell like that."

"What would it smell like?"

"I'm not going to tell you."

"Well, I know I smell something. Could there be a short in the wiring for the thermostat or something?"

With a look of long-suffering on his face, he got up and checked the furnace.

"There's not a thing wrong here!"

I smelled rubber all evening, and after everyone had gone to bed I checked all the burners on the stove and the electrical outlets, but I couldn't find the smell. Then I remembered. I had put a pair of tennis shoes on the hot water tank to dry. I knew I smelled something.

"Do not be anxious about anything, but in everything, by prayer . . . present your requests to God. And the peace of God . . . will guard your hearts and minds in Christ Jesus" (Phil. 4:6,7).

How can we convince anyone we trust the Lord if we worry all the time?

COUPON SALE

LAST WEEK ONE OF THE MARKETS ACROSS town was having its grand opening and some of its sale prices (with coupons) were unbelievable. So I clipped the coupons, found the location on a street map, and planned to leave early enough in the morning to be there when the doors opened.

It was raining the next morning, but what was a little rain when I could save so much on groceries? I was waiting at the door when the manager unlocked it, and I pushed my way in, ahead of two other early shoppers.

It was a huge store. Long aisles of merchandise stretched before me like a giant maze. I felt dwarfed and confused. How would I ever find all the things on my list? I got a basket, started at one wall, and began to work my way back and forth. Everything looked so good! I probably should have eaten breakfast, because when I was about halfway through the store my basket was full, and I hadn't found one item on my list. I looked at the Oreo cookies, shrimp cocktail, and canned asparagus in my basket. No more goodies for me, I decided. I would find those sale items and leave.

150

The store was out of the coffee it had advertised, and the turkeys were all thirty pounds or more. I got a ham (which was not a sale item) and a few other things at the meat counter. Then, struggling with an overloaded basket, I finally found all the coupon items — cat and dog food, sugar, rice, beans — I don't remember what all, but I figured with the coupons I would be saving about seven dollars. Triumphantly, I lumbered up to the check-out counter.

"Good-morning!" the bright-eyed checker sang out. The computerized cash register began to make refined cricket chirps. The tally was $52.37 and my hand trembled as I began to write the check. Thank goodness I had the coupons. When I presented them to her she looked sad and bit her lower lip.

"Oh, I *am* sorry! These won't be good until tomorrow!"

As I put the groceries in the trunk I felt depressed. By the time I got home I would have used a lot of gas, and I knew I had spent at least ten dollars more by trying to save money in that new store than if I had shopped in my own area.

<hr />

"If any of you lacks wisdom, he should ask of God, who gives generously to all without finding fault, and it will be given to him" (James 1:5).

". . . . Satan himself masquerades as an angel of light" (2 Cor. 11:14).

We need to watch and be alert, because some bargains are too expensive — and the devil's merchandise is always on sale.

151

MOTHER'S LITTLE HELPER

MY FOLKS ALWAYS TAUGHT US TO DO OUR share of work. In our family it was a sin to be idle.

"And when you go visiting," my mother counseled, "always help do the housework and dishes. And look around for other ways to be helpful."

This advice got me into trouble last month when I visited my sister-in-law. The first day I was there we had planned to go shopping, so while she took a shower and got dressed, I did the breakfast dishes. I noticed the dog's dish was empty so I fed him. I didn't know the bacon grease and a piece of bread would make him throw up in the bedroom.

In the living room I noticed the plant on the coffee table was bone dry, so I watered it, being extra careful not to get one drop on the table.

The next morning I heard my sister-in-law let out a scream.

"Who watered this plant?"

I came running from my room and she was waving a wet Bible in her hand.

"It's ruined!" she screeched. "Absolutely ruined!" The

coffee table had a big white spot on it, too. How could I have known the planter was made of unfired clay and would leak in the night? I offered to buy her a new Bible, but she kept shaking her head and whimpering.

Later she insisted on doing the dishes herself, but I wanted to help her get the work done, so she finally gave me a dustcloth. While dusting her desk, I saw a few letters with stamps on them, so I put them out in the mailbox.

When she was opening her mail I said,

"Oh, by the way, I mailed your letters on the desk."

"You *what?*" She had that wild look in her eyes again.

"The letters. I mailed them. Did I do something wrong?" She groaned.

"Not if you can loan me one hundred dollars until Friday."

"Huh?"

"That's about how much it will take to cover the checks you mailed."

Surely mother is right about helping, but in my case it's probably better if I sit back and let others help me.

" . . . *every fool will be meddling*" (Prov. 20:3 KJV).

We ought to use the brains God has given us — but thankfully, our salvation doesn't depend on it.

SPOOKED

IT'S ALMOST HALLOWE'EN AGAIN. I EN-
joy handing out treats to the children, but I'm worried
about the tricks my family may play on me.

Last year my son said,

"One of the neighbors told me that a long time ago
somebody died in our house."

"Oh, no!"

"Yeah. Said they couldn't get the coffin out through the
hall, so they took it out the window."

"Oooh!" I shuddered.

"Said because of that, the spirit will never rest and
comes back on Hallowe'en."

"Oh, stop!"

"They say sometimes you can hear a window opening
and shutting — "

"Please — "

" — and there's moaning and groaning — "

I put my fingers in my ears.

All during dinner my family kept scaring me.

"Did you hear that window open?" one of them
whispered.

"Wonder who found the body? Maybe it was murder!"

Later in the evening, when I went out to the kitchen to get a snack, my husband was waiting for me. His arms were raised high above his head, monster-fashion, his eyes were crossed, and his hair hung down over his eyes. But worst of all, he had carved two long fangs out of a potato and had them stuck under his upper lip. I knew it was him, but I began to scream and beat him on the chest. I couldn't seem to control myself. Finally, with my arms pinned to my sides, he got me calmed down and promised he wouldn't do that again. But he kept laughing at me while he ate his fangs.

I wonder what tricks my family has planned for me this year? I ought to beat them to it and scare *them*. I could make myself a ghoul costume and get a witch wig and a horror mask, and sprinkle dirt on me like I'd just come out of the grave. I could have catsup dripping from my hands and go out in the dark and tap on a bedroom window and moan and — *ooo-ooh!* I've got *myself* scared!

"Do not be afraid of sudden panic . . . for the LORD *will be your confidence . . ."* (Prov. 3:25,26).

"I sought the LORD, *and he answered me, and delivered me from all my fears"* (Ps. 34:4).

There is nothing the Lord cannot take care of, including our every fear.

WINDOW PAIN

I THINK THERE SHOULD BE A LAW AGAINST commercials that claim certain products make window cleaning easy. There's no such thing as easy window cleaning. It's a back-breaking, finger-wrecking job, and that's why I keep my living room drapes closed when I have company.

Yesterday morning I opened the drapes to see what the weather was like and thought there must be a smog alert. But after I wrote my name on the window, I realized the time had come to either wash windows or leave the lights on all day. I took a good look at my drapes, too, and saw they were no longer "wheat beige" but more like "potato brown." In a foolish spurt of enthusiasm, I took them down and crammed them into the washing machine. Before I could change my mind, I hurried into the living room and sprayed all the windows with a liquid "sure-clean" product. But I should have dusted the window sills first because I soon had mud puddles to clean up.

After I had rubbed the panes until both arms ached and the tips of my fingers were sore, I went outside and turned the hose on the windows; but after they dried they were

156

more streaked and spotted than before. Besides that, somehow the water got inside, made a dirty streak down the wall, and soaked the carpet. But I was determined to have sparkling clean windows, so I got the ladder, took off the screens, and used a cream-type, "easy-clean" product on the outside.

While it dried, I checked on the drapes and found that the hooks had come out during washing and were stuck in the holes in the tub. Unfortunately there were also many rips in the drapes. After I put them in the dryer, I opened the sewing machine.

Outside, with a big towel in hand, I tripped lightly up the ladder to start polishing. The water from the hose had softened the ground considerably and one side of the ladder began to sink. I felt very foolish lying in the mud, but after I got up I put a brick under the ladder and finished the job. (I ignored the drops of water I flipped on the windows when I put the screens back.)

This morning I yanked the drapes back to let the sunshine in, and there were all the streaks, spots, and spatters I had missed. Slowly, I closed the drapes. Happily, the mended places in the drapes hardly show.

"Create in me a clean heart, O God, and put a new and right spirit within me" (Ps. 51:10).

" . . . and the blood of Jesus, his Son, purifies us from every sin" (1 John 1:7).

When we try to clean up our lives by our own efforts we find they are still streaked and smeared with sin. Only fellowship with Christ will keep us clean.

157

UNWANTED GIFT

ON CHRISTMAS, BIRTHDAYS, AND MOTHER'S Day I find out what an ungrateful person I really am. But honestly, doesn't it seem reasonable to hope that if you give out all kinds of hints you'd get what you want?

Before my birthday last year I kept hinting to the whole family that I love perfume, but didn't have any, not even any bath powder.

"You'll make me happy with *anything* that smells good," I said.

My daughter gave me a box of chocolates.

"Nothing smells as good as chocolate," she defended.

My son gave me a spice rack, complete with twelve bottes of spices.

"Smell this Italian seasoning!" he exclaimed. "Smells just like pizza!"

Before Christmas I told them I wanted clothes. I cut out pictures of blouses and slacks and pinned them to the kitchen curtain. I made a point of flapping the loose sole of my bedroom slipper when anyone came near me, and scratched my leg through a tear in my jeans.

One of the kids gave me a T-shirt. It was the right size,

but I'd rather not wear it. It has a monster face on it with the words *Horror You?*

My son gave me a beautiful pair of black kid gloves, but I haven't worn size five since *I* was five, and he couldn't remember where he bought them.

My husband, bless him, gave me a beautiful, black imitation fur coat, but he must have gotten my hip size mixed up with my dress size, because it reaches to my ankles.

When I got my ears pierced, I was sure I would get earrings for Mother's Day. I did — the slip-on kind.

It's hard not to feel irritated with my family about some of the dumb things they give me. I've never asked for an electric glue gun or a Fonz jigsaw puzzle. After all, I really try to give them things they want, or at least things that I know are best for them. They aren't too grateful, either. On my daughter's birthday she complained that she really wanted Levis instead of red polka-dot pants. At Christmas my son said pajamas and bathrobe were okay, but he'd hoped to get a guitar. My husband hasn't taken his shirt and tie out of the box — and it's summer. Maybe he was being sarcastic when he said he loved clothes.

This Christmas I think I'm going to ask for a saw, a bicycle pump, and a rake. Maybe I'll get something I want.

"Every good and perfect gift is from above, coming down from the Father . . . " (James 1:17).

We may not like some gifts, but we can receive them with gratefulness and love for the giver.

159

GESUNDHEIT!

THEY ANNOUNCED ON THE NEWS LAST night that there's a new flu virus going around. I guess it's pretty serious, but I wish they wouldn't broadcast things like that. Makes a person uneasy — you can't help but worry that you might get it. If somebody sneezes in a crowd, immediately you wonder, "Has he got it?"

The other day I met a friend in the store. She kept coughing and blowing her nose, and I couldn't even concentrate on what she was saying because I was trying to smile, lean back, and hold my breath all at the same time. It gave me the creeps just imagining how many germs were billowing out of her and trying to get into me. Of course I try never to let those things really bother me. You just have to apply mind over matter. (However, I did gargle as soon as I got home.)

I have a relative who gets everything she hears about. The minute she hears of some new ailment, she begins to have the symptoms. When she goes to the doctor, it's for a confirmation of her own diagnosis. You watch, as soon as she hears about this new flu, she'll get it — and she won't call it the flu. She'll call it by its medical name. She always uses long, medical terms. I remember one summer she had a few bumps on her arm, and when I asked her what it was, instead of saying "just a little rash," she said she had "dermatitis repense." And she never gets anything as ordinary as a "toothache." It's always "impacted" or worse. And then it's never "pulled." She has "oral surgery."

I guess she can't help it if she's a hypochondriac. But I'm thankful I'm not like that. I'm hardly ever sick; and if I don't feel well, I try not to talk about it. Ignore your ailments, I always say. Of course, there are times when you can't ignore how you feel. Like right now my head is aching, my chest feels tight, and my nose feels like it might start running. Phooey. Those are the symptoms of that new flu.

The newscaster said not to take chances, and although I don't want to be a baby, I think I'll go right to bed. I'm sure I have some dreadful *febrile zymotic* disorder.

"Why do you look at the speck of sawdust in your brother's eye and pay no attention to the plank in your own eye?" (Matt. 7:3).

"For in the same way you judge others, you will be judged, and with the measure you use, it will be measured to you" (Matt. 7:2).

Why is it we find fault with others, yet justify and excuse the same thing in ourselves?

GREEN EYES

WE HAD BEEN INVITED TO MY HUSBAND'S employer's home for a Christmas party and dinner. Since there were twenty-four people, there were several tables, and his wife had a diabolical seating system. The women chose red numbers out of a dish, while the men chose green. Each person had to find his or her corresponding color and number at a table. I found my place between two old boys who were due to retire, while my husband was seated back in a corner with two cute secretaries and a salesman.

The dinner was fantastic, but I couldn't enjoy it. I kept wondering what was going on at my husband's table. I did try to talk to my dinner companions, but it was like pushing the vacuum across a shag carpet on "low."

"It's been hot for December," I said.

"How's that?"

"Hot for December."

"Hotter in thirty-three."

I turned to the other man.

"What sort of work do you do?"

"Pardon?"

"What do you do at the company?"

"Oh! As little as possible! Ho, ho, ho, ho."

I looked at my husband and he was laughing too, and pounding on the table. One of the girls slapped him on the arm and howled. Later on in the meal he looked serious and leaned close to her. She looked serious too. What could they be talking about? I had never seen him look so appealing — except when he had asked me to marry him. I was miserable. I don't even remember what they served for dessert, I was so jealous.

After dinner I told him I was sick and wanted to go. I didn't speak to him on the way home. In bed when he leaned over to kiss me good-night, I turned my face away. He snapped on the light and saw my tears.

"What's the matter with you?"

"You know what's the matter."

"I *don't* know. You tell me."

"You're in love with her, aren't you?"

"Who? What are you talking about?"

"Her! Her! I saw you drooling over her during dinner."

A look of understanding came over his face.

"You mean Flossie?" Then he looked angry. "Well, now you've ruined it. You and your jealousy."

"What do you mean?"

"My Christmas surprise. Now I'll have to tell you. Flossie's husband is a jeweler, and I've ordered a new set of rings for you. I hope you're satisfied." He flounced over on his side.

I was very ashamed. I cried until I had the hiccups. However, there is one happy thought — I won't know what the rings look like until Christmas morning.

"For jealousy is the rage of a man . . ." (Prov. 6:34 κJV).

"For where you have envy and selfish ambition, there you find disorder and every evil practice" (James 3:16).

Jealous words and actions never produce the love we want.

FLIGHT 425

WHEN I GOT OFF THE PLANE THE OTHER night, I had the feeling the hostess was glad to see me go.

Before the plane ever left the ground, she seemed to be provoked at me. I had put my overnight case in the storage compartment up front; then, after I was seated in the last row, I decided it would be a good idea to get some of the tracts out of it. After all, the pastor said to be a good witness. It must have been a little disturbing to have me fight my way forward in the narrow aisle while people were still boarding, and this particular hostess shook her head and moaned slightly as I squeezed past her.

The flight attendants served drinks as soon as we were in the air, and it wasn't long after I'd finished my Seven-Up until they came around collecting the cups and glasses. I gave her my glass but kept a big ice cube. After awhile I got tired of a frozen mouth, so when the hostess came toward me with a cup in her hand, I smiled at her and dropped the ice cube in the cup. She looked startled and a little bit cross.

"That wasn't a dirty cup," she said through gritted teeth. "I was getting a passenger a refill." I felt terrible! I apologized and determined not to get into any more trouble.

I tried to go to sleep, but my shoes were too tight. I took them off and tucked them back under my seat, stretched my toes, and relaxed. I had the aisle seat, and I relaxed more than I realized, because my head lolled out in the aisle. Wouldn't you know that same hostess bumped into it? She was carrying a couple of dinner trays and almost lost her balance. She stopped and looked down at me with a peculiar expression, almost as though she was angry.

Soon it was my turn to get a dinner tray, and the food was delicious. When she came to pick up my tray, she eyed me warily.

"Are you through?"

"Yes," I said; but just as she reached for the tray, I decided to have one more sip of coffee.

"Oh, no!" she wailed as she looked at the coffee on my white slacks. "Just sit still. I'll be right back."

When she returned, she had a can of pop in her hand and dumped about half of it in my lap. It was ice cold.

"It's club soda," she said. "It'll take the stain right out." She mopped vigorously. I felt so stupid. She tipped the can up and poured out some more. I took the towel away from her.

"Please don't worry," I said. "It was my fault."

"I know. But you don't want coffee stains on that suit."

When the pilot announced we'd be landing in about ten minutes, I started to put on my shoes. One was missing. I asked the fellow across the aisle if he could see it. He barely glanced under my seat and shook his head. I don't think he wanted to have anything to do with me.

As much as I hated to, I had to get down on my hands and knees in the aisle to look for my other shoe. I was in a knee-chest position when I heard a familiar voice say,

"What now?"

I held up my shoe and smiled apologetically. With two trays held high she stepped over me.

When I got off the plane, she was saying nice things to all the passengers:

"So glad you were on board."

"It was a pleasure to have you."

"Please fly with us again." But when she saw me, she simply said,

"Good-by."

I completely forgot about giving her a tract.

"In everything set them an example by doing what is good. In . . . integrity, seriousness . . . so that those who oppose you may . . . have nothing bad to say of us" (Titus 2:7,8).

We should always be ready to share our faith, but our good witness can be canceled by thoughtless actions.

AFTER ITS KIND

TWO YEARS AGO IN THE SPRING, I FELL IN love with twelve yellow powder puffs with beaks. When I placed the box of peeping baby chicks on the living room carpet, my husband raised a few questions:

"What do you know about growing chickens? Where will you keep them? Won't they eat an awful lot? Won't the little kids let them get into our garden? Aren't chickens dirty? Don't they crow a lot? Will the neighbors complain?"

But, cuddling them in my hands, I didn't have any answers.

For the first two weeks they slept in our spare bedroom, in a big box with a heating pad. Meanwhile, as enthusiastic as an expectant mother, I cleaned and painted the old chicken house already on our property.

In a short time the chickens were broiler size, and my husband suggested we eat them. I hardly spoke to him for a week after that. But looking back, I realize he had a good idea, because by that time they were large, white vultures that wanted to eat *us*. Every time I took food to them, they would fly up at me and knock the pan out of my hand. I

168

soon learned not to wear sandals at feeding time. I guess they thought my toes were fat worms.

My husband had been right. Dirty! You wouldn't believe. Noisy! And the kids *did* let them out, and they practically ruined the garden in one afternoon. Neighbors complained after one of the hens turned out to be a rooster who crowed at 3:00 A.M. They ate constantly. If I didn't keep enough food in the feeder, they attacked each other.

One day after an unearthly shrieking, I ran out to the chicken yard, and there was a big, white egg! My babies were beginning to lay. Ecstatic, I ran in to get my camera, but before I could take a picture of the egg, one of the other hens ate it.

A few weeks ago I noticed the worst-tempered hen wouldn't get off the nest. Every time I tried to get the eggs from under her, she pecked my arm. After several chicken bites I let her alone.

And then one morning last week I went out to feed the little monsters, and there, peeking out of the crabby hen's feathers, was a yellow powder puff. She hatched nine babies and they're adorable. As I watch her clucking and leading them around, tears come to my eyes. Does this make me "grandchicken"?

"And God created . . . every winged fowl after his kind; and God saw that it was good" (Gen. 1:21 KJV).

It may be fashionable to believe in evolution — but only God could *create* a baby chick.

MERCHANTS

NEIGHBORS DOWN THE STREET WERE having a garage sale, and one evening after dinner my husband and I strolled down to see what they had. I was amazed at how brisk business was for them. While we were there, some people bought an old floor lamp, and teenagers bought some old Indian jewelry. There were several people milling around, and I began to feel worried we might miss out on a bargain.

"Let's buy this bookcase," I whispered to my husband. "It's only five dollars."

"Okay," he agreed. "It'll be just right for those *Reader's Digest Condensed Books* over there. Can you believe they're only fifty cents each?"

"There's more merchandise inside," the lady said. It was fun to go into a strange house and have a legitimate excuse to snoop around. She had clothing for sale, and there were tags on almost all the furniture. I decided to buy a beautiful set of dishes for only five dollars. True, there weren't any cups, but I was sure I could find some to match. My husband bought a saw and some other tools. When we got home, we were shocked when we realized we had spent twenty-five dollars!

"A severe case of impulse buying," my husband observed sadly.

"Why don't *we* have a garage sale?" I said. "Just think of the stuff we've got that we never use! How about that old ladder? And our old lounge chairs on the patio?" We ran an ad in the local paper and got all our stuff tagged and arranged attractively on the driveway and patio.

People began to come early the day of the sale, even before I had dressed. Our first customers were three burly men in a truck. They stamped up the driveway and strode through the patio. I went out to meet them in my bathrobe.

"Is this all you've got?" one man asked.

"Well, no," I said, feeling intimidated. "There's a little bit in the house." They walked boldly through the kitchen and into the dining room.

"What are you asking for the hutch?"

"Uh, well, I — "

"Give you seventy-five," the biggest man said.

"We aren't selling any of our furniture," my husband spoke up.

"Thought you were having a sale!" They turned in disgust.

I went to bedroom to dress, and suddenly a woman appeared at the door.

"Is your ironing board for sale?"

I shrugged. Why not?

"How about three dollars?" I suggested.

She gave me the money and picked up the ironing board in one quick motion. She ran down the hall like a surfer to the beach.

I looked at the money in my hand. I had made a sale! Confident now, I went to greet the public like an experienced storekeeper. In quick succession I sold the vacuum sweeper, a set of dishes (with cups), and the kitchen table and chairs. Meanwhile my husband had sold our black-and-white TV and his lawn mower and edger. And we kept selling things all day.

When evening came, we were worn out and had not sold the old ladder or any of the old lounging chairs. We had $180, but it would take $500 to replace what we'd sold.

"I've never heard of it before," my husband said, "but I guess we had a severe case of impulse *selling.*"

"The plans of the diligent lead surely to abundance, but every one who is hasty comes only to want" (Prov. 21:5).

"For the love of money is a root of all kinds of evil. Some people, eager for money, have wandered from the faith and pierced themselves with many griefs" (1 Tim. 6:10).

If we're too eager to get our hands on a few dollars, we could get our souls into a lot of trouble.

TRIAL BY TURKEY

OF ALL THE THINGS I HAVE TO BE THANK-ful for, I think I'm most thankful that this won't be my first family Thanksgiving dinner. What a nightmare that day was! In the past all our family had either gone to my mother's house or my sister's for Thanksgiving dinner, but that year I decided it was my turn.

As I looked at the naked, thirty-pound turkey in the sink, I was appalled. I alone was responsible for getting the pin feathers out, the stuffing in, and that bird baked. He was a miserable sight. His tail was tucked inside in a humiliating way and fastened to his legs with an immoveable piece of wire. I think he must have been deformed because his neck was down in his chest cavity. I felt a wave of nausea as I explored his insides. I wanted to cry out for help, but I knew I had to do it all alone.

The menu called for giblet gravy, per my mother's recipe, but I couldn't find the giblets until dinnertime when my husband carved. There were the gizzard, heart, and liver neatly stashed in a paper bag in a flap of skin near its throat. Apparently the paper bag helped to cook them, because they were the only parts of the fowl that were

173

done. A pink liquid squirted out wherever my husband inserted the knife. There was nothing to do but put the thing back in the oven, but the family didn't think the extra hour delay was amusing. They kept circling the table; and by the time the turkey was done, all the olives, pickles, and celery were gone.

When it was time to eat, somebody pulled on one end of the table to make more room at the other end, and part of the dinner fell into the gap where the leaves go. We put paper towels over the messy places on the table cloth, and after a blessing that took much faith, we began to eat.

The turkey was actually pretty good, but the dressing was pale and about the consistency of overcooked Cream of Wheat. Later, the pumpkin pie was slurpy — undercooked, of course. I just don't know how that could have happened either, because the crust was burned.

So, I have a lot to be thankful for this Thanksgiving. Mainly that we'll be going to my sister's house for dinner. I don't know if I'll ever have the courage to go through that responsibility by myself again.

"Always giving thanks to God the Father for everything, in the name of our Lord Jesus Christ" (Eph. 5:20).

"God has said, 'Never will I leave you; never will I forsake you.' So we say with confidence, 'The Lord is my helper . . . ' " (Heb. 13:5,6).

How thankful we can be that we don't have to go through anything without His presence.

FORTUNE TELLER

I FELT GUILTY WHEN I AGREED TO GO WITH my friend Louise to Madam Vanessa's Tea Room. I was brought up to stay away from fortune tellers, mediums, and any kind of witchcraft.

"But what can it hurt?" Louise coaxed. "I've always wanted to have my fortune told and I don't want to go alone." She frowned a little. "Besides, we get our lunch with the price of the reading."

I was surprised and disappointed when we found the address in an office building downtown. There were no black curtains or any candles burning, only a brightly lit lobby. A hostess in an ordinary pantsuit took us to a table. Lattice-work partitions divided the booths, but aside from that we could have been in any little cafe. However, there wasn't a menu. A waitress brought us the dinkiest tuna sandwiches I have ever seen, one olive, three potato chips, and a pot of tea.

After we had eaten, Madam Vanessa came to our table. Again I was surprised and disappointed. I thought she would be wearing a turban, a diamond glued to her forehead, and be dressed in gypsy clothes, but she looked like a middle-aged model. Her hair was pulled back in a knot and her lips were painted bright red. She had on large, gold hoop earrings, and a slender chain adorned her navy blue dress.

"Good afternoon, ladies," she said with a slight accent. She didn't smile. "Do you wish tea-leaf reading, crystal ball, or palm? Perhaps cards?"

"Does one cost any more than the other?" I asked.

"Certainly not!" She looked at me contemptuously.

"Not cards," I said. "The Bible admonishes us to avoid the appearance of evil." I folded my hands primly. "I'll have a palm reading."

Louise chose the crystal ball, and Madam Vanessa told hers first. I don't remember everything she told Louise, but she did say,

"Beware of one you call friend," and turned to me coldly. She took both my hands and turned them palm up. She began to trace lines with her bony forefinger and I had to grit my teeth to keep from giggling because it tickled.

"The most important man in your life is blond and handsome."

I smiled. I *knew* this stuff was phony. My husband has dark hair and, well, attractive maybe.

"You have had a great tragedy in your life."

The worst thing that's ever happened to me was when I broke out with measles during my sixteenth birthday party.

"Beware of a gift from your mother-in-law."

I almost laughed in her face. My husband's mother is dead.

She folded my hand into a fist and looked at the creases.

"You have two children and will bear a third."

I gasped. Good grief, maybe there is something to fortune telling. I *do* have two children.

"Then Saul said to his servants, 'Seek out for me a woman who is a medium, that I may go to her and inquire of her'" (1 Sam. 28:7).

"So Saul died for his unfaithfulness; he was unfaithful to the Lord *in that he did not keep the command of the* Lord, *and also consulted a medium, seeking guidance"* (1 Chron. 10:13).

We insult the Lord when we go to a fortune teller and that is dangerous. Besides, their counsel cannot bring peace to our hearts.

A NEW DIVINITY

ONE OF MY FRIENDS MAKES THE BEST divinity fudge I've ever eaten. She gave us several pieces along with some other Christmas goodies, and my husband and I almost fought over the last piece.

"Why don't you ever make divinity?" he asked.

"I've tried, but it's always a failure."

"Why not get her recipe?" So I called her.

"Be sure you have a candy thermometer," she said, "and try to pick a time when there isn't any dampness in the air."

I waited for a bright sunny day and then I started "Operation Divinity."

Her recipe was so simple I wondered why I had been afraid to try it. When the sugar spun a six-inch thread (which floated up into my hair), I folded in the stiff egg whites, and then the nuts and vanilla. It was stiff and hard to work, just like the recipe said it would be. I patted it into a glass dish and waited for it to cool so I could cut it into thick, yummy squares.

About an hour later I decided to cut it. The knife bounced out of my hand. I couldn't even stick the point of the knife in, and yet the white mass quivered like Jello. I waited another hour but it was like tar on a warm day. I called my friend.

"Hmm," she murmured. "Mine is always ready to cut almost as soon as I put it in the pan. If it's still soft after two hours I'm afraid there's not much you can do. Pass out spoons!" She laughed.

"Not funny," I said. "Three cups of sugar, three eggs, and a whole cup of pecans."

"Try making it into balls and then rolling them in powdered sugar."

"Good idea!" I hurried back to the kitchen, washed my hands, and started making round balls. When I rolled them in powdered sugar they looked delicious. I ate one. It was delicious. I had a whole platter full of round balls, and I covered them with plastic and put them in the refrigerator.

When I started to offer some to my husband that night the platter was full of white tar, and running off the edges.

"About all you can do with it is frost a cake," my friend advised.

I baked a chocolate oblong cake. The divinity made nice icing, but I still couldn't cut it. I rolled cake and icing up like a log, wrapped it in foil, and put it on the table. It got longer and flatter and pretty soon white lava oozed out onto the table. By this time the whole family knew of my failure.

"That stuff's growing," my husband commented. "You'd better throw it out before it takes over the earth."

As a last attempt to save it I poured two cups of powdered sugar on the cake and kneaded it until it was so stiff it wouldn't move a fraction of a centimeter. With a sharp knife I cut it into squares. Although it was the color of a palamino horse, it was delicious!

I served it with pride Christmas Eve.

"Tremendous!" my family said.

179

"Delicious!"
"Get the recipe!"

" . . . Joseph said . . . you meant evil against me; but God meant it for good . . . " (Gen. 50:19,20).

"But thanks be to God, who always leads us in triumphal procession in Christ . . ." (2 Cor. 2:14).

We can look back on our Christian experience and see that God meant each trial for good. We can look to the future triumphantly!

LAST WILL AND TESTAMENT

MY AUNT STAYED WITH US FOR A WHILE after my uncle died, and she impressed upon me the importance of making a will.

"Your uncle could have saved us such a lot of heartache and bickering if he'd made an explicit will," she complained. "His brothers are fighting over who should get his shotgun and his silver dollar collection, and I don't know who should get his Hamilton watch when I'm gone." She snuffled sadly. "But as soon as I get home, I'm going to make my will, right down to my jewelry and antiques."

I got to looking around at my valuables and decided she was right, so I drew up my will.

1. All my trading stamps, both loose and in books, are to go to my sister. (I think I still owe her two and a half books anyway.)

2. My half-used Disneyland coupon books, even the one from 1969, are to go to my son, to use any way he sees fit.

3. Both my paint-by-number pictures are to be given to my mother, who always said I had talent.

4. The cookbook I've used since we were married I will

181

to my daughter. Although it hasn't helped me, it probably won't hurt her.

5. My permanent curlers are to be given to my cousin, who poodle's hair turned straight after her first litter.

6. All my Avon perfume bottles I bequeath to my niece, a true antique lover.

7. My Tupperware, including lids, I give to my neighbor, because she always has a huge garden and lots of leftovers.

8. My class ring I leave to my youngest nephew. He may need to hock it someday.

9. My wedding ring I will to my beloved husband, although if he ever gets rid of me, I doubt he'd be willing to take another shot at marriage.

Thanks, auntie, for advice well taken.

"Do not store up for yourselves treasures on earth, where moth and rust destroy, and where thieves break in and steal" (Matt. 6:19).

"What good will it be for a man if he gains the whole world, yet forfeits his soul?" (Matt. 16:26).

The more we have here on earth, the less interest we seem to have in heaven.

TROUBLES, TRIBULATIONS

ONE NIGHT ABOUT NINE-THIRTY MY HUS-
band said, "You know what I'd really like to eat? Pizza!"

"Oh, yes!" I agreed. "All that hot melted cheese!"

About half an hour later he walked in, a disappointed
look on his face, and a paper sack in his hand.

"Zipanni's closes at nine — and I couldn't find any other
place around here." He opened the sack. "So I got a
couple of hot dogs."

"Too bad," I said as I bit into mine. "I had some in the
refrigerator."

A few nights later when he got home from work I said,

"I've been working hard all day. Could we go out for a
Chinese dinner?"

"Great! I've been hungry for Chinese food. Canton
Palace?"

When we got there a sign in the door read, "Closed
Tuesdays."

"Rats!" I cried. "Can you believe this?"

"Do you know of any other Chinese restaurant?"

"No. We might as well go home."

"How about hamburgers?" one of the kids suggested.

Hamburgers and French fries are fine, but not when you have your stomach all set for shrimp chow mein and egg rolls.

For my husband's birthday I decided to treat him to his favorite: prime rib. I wouldn't try to cook it, but we would go to Lord Rodney's, and I would pay for it with my egg money. When I told him my plan, he said,

"Better call and make sure they'll be open."

I did and made reservations. And I called a sitter.

When the waitress came to our table with menus, my husband said,

"We won't need those. We both want prime rib."

"Oh, I'm sorry, sir," she said. "We only serve prime rib on the weekend."

He shook his head sadly.

"I wonder what day of the week my birthday falls on next year?"

But it turned out okay. Their special that night was spaghetti and meatballs, served with a slice of pizza.

"This poor man cried, and the LORD heard him, and saved him out of all his troubles" (Ps. 34:6).

"I have told you these things, so that in me you may have peace. In this world you will have trouble. But take heart! I have overcome the world" (John 16:33).

There won't be so many disappointments in life if we can learn not to have our hearts set on anything except Jesus Christ.

SUPER-DUPER FUTURE

MY FOLKS ARE ALWAYS TALKING ABOUT "the good old days," but I think people are prone to look backward when they're too old to look forward. Just think how amazing this world is right now and how there are even more exciting things ahead. The Bible says that in the end times knowledge will be increased (Dan. 12:4).

Wouldn't it be wonderful if some shoe manufacturer would come up with shoes that would last children a whole year? Maybe they could have some kind of flexible, light-weight metal soles and stretchable plastic tops — and shoelaces that would never break!

Also, I'm looking forward to the day some smart doctor invents a weight-pacer you could have installed in your stomach. All you'd have to do is set the dial on 120 pounds, or whatever you want to weigh, and it would automatically regulate your desires about food. "No, thanks," you'd hear yourself saying, "for some reason pecan pie doesn't appeal to me."

In the future maybe Detroit will invent a spray that you squirt on the fenders of your car that will cause other cars to be repelled. If everybody used it, fender-benders would be completely eliminated.

And speaking of sprays, wouldn't it be fantastic to be able to spray all the dishes after a meal with a food remover (nonpoisonous, of course), and all the dishes and silverware would be clean and ready to put away? We could even leave them on the table for the next meal. Terrific!

Homemakers need a device under the bed, with strings fastened to the corners of the covers. Then we could simply step on a pedal and presto! our bed would be made.

How about a machine (there could be several at each post office) that you place your address book in, along with your Christmas cards, and it would automatically address, seal, and stamp the envelopes?

Wow! When there are so many things ahead, why would we want to look back?

———

" . . . Forgetting what is behind and straining toward what is ahead . . ." (Phil. 3:13).

" . . . while we wait for the blessed hope — the glorious appearing of our great God and Savior, Jesus Christ" (Titus 2:13).

The greatest thing ahead is our future life with *Him*. Maybe He'll come for us today!

GOOFY TWO SHOES

MY SISTER HAD BEEN VISITING US, AND I had to take her to the bus depot downtown. Since we left home before dawn, I had dressed in the dark, because there was no need to wake my husband that early.

While standing in the ticket line, I glanced at my feet and couldn't believe what I saw. I was wearing one white shoe and one tan shoe. They weren't even the same style. If only I could hide my feet! I thought of squatting down, but I knew that would attract even more attention. I poked my sister.

"Look at my feet."

Frowning, she looked down. Her mouth dropped open. She looked up at me with wide eyes and sucked in her breath. Then she threw back her head and laughed — a wild, insane whooping that made everyone turn and stare. I folded my arms carelessly and looked around. Sis got control of herself and stared straight ahead, but her shoulders kept jumping up and down convulsively.

My mind groped for a solution. Could I take my shoes off and walk around in my stocking feet? Maybe people would think I was a celebrity. Or why not tie a handkerchief around one foot and limp? Maybe if I could just stand with my feet far enough apart, people wouldn't notice. The line moved up, and I took one giant step forward with the tan shoe and left the white foot behind. I stood poised like a runner for a moment, but lost my balance and had to grab my sister to keep from falling.

After she got her ticket, we walked to the cafeteria to get breakfast. I squared my shoulders haughtily and lifted my chin as we walked across the block-wide waiting room. I couldn't have felt more conspicuous if my feet had been in red plaster casts.

Later, while we waited for the bus, I leaned non-chalantly against the wall and tucked one foot up under my dress like a flamingo. When it was time to go, the gatekeeper let me walk out to the bus with my sister, and the last time I saw her through the bus window she was out of control, laughing and wiping tears and pointing at my feet.

In my car I took off my shoes and put them on the seat. They didn't look too bad together. I remembered my tan-and-white flowered dress and thought how nice they'd look with it. Maybe I could start a new fad.

" . . . for the Lord sees not as man sees; man looks on the outward appearance, but the LORD looks on the heart" (1 Sam. 16:7).

"Stop judging by mere appearances, but make a right judgment" (John 7:24).

We worry so much about how we look to others, when the main thing is to be concerned about how we appear to God.

188

QUIET PLEASE!

"WHY DID YOU SAY YOU WANTED ME TO help you change bedrooms with Joanie?" my husband asked one Saturday morning.

"Because of Billy next door and his motorcycle. That thing wakes me every time he comes in or out of the driveway."

"That's funny. I never hear him," my husband remarked.

That wasn't surprising, I thought. He had never heard either of the babies cry in the night, or the dog bark, or the phone ring.

"Well, his noise is just terrible," I said. "And I told him off yesterday."

"You didn't!"

"Yes, I did." I lifted my chin defiantly. "I told him I thought he ought to have more consideration for us."

He shook his head sadly, and I knew he was ashamed of me. I was ashamed of myself, but that racket had made me lose control.

"So, now the plan is for us to move all the furniture from our room to Joanie's and vice versa?" I nodded. "Okay.

189

Let's start by putting all her furniture out in the hall." He got a grip on her mattress. "Tip your end to the left," he ordered. I did, and twisted it out of his hands.

"To the left!" he shouted.

"This *is* left!" I shouted back.

"I meant *my* left!" We got the mattress off the bed and started out the door. "Now just back out of the room and down the hall — no, no, don't turn! I'll swing my end up."

"Up? Does it have to stand on end?"

"I didn't mean up in the air," he gritted. We left the mattress in the hall and went back for the springs. I knew which way to tilt it this time; but as we lifted it up, I saw something gleam under a layer of fuzz.

"My good scissors!" I yelped and dropped my end of the springs. He lost his balance and knocked over the lamp. His lips began to move strangely, and I knew he was counting to ten. "I'm sorry, honey, but these scissors have been lost for weeks. How do you suppose they got under the bed?"

"I could make a cutting remark," he said, "but come on, we'll never get through."

Two hours and several misunderstandings later the job was finished. I was looking forward to a quiet night and Joanie was excited about her new room. But I was afraid she might not sleep well, either. The next morning I asked her if Billy's cycle had kept her awake. She shook her head.

"He didn't make any noise 'cause he pushed it up the driveway."

"You mean he didn't roar up and gun it over and over?"

"No, he was quiet as a mouse. He said he didn't want to disturb you."

I haven't been sleeping too well lately. I don't know if it's the traffic noise from the street, or my conscience.

190

"Be wise in the way you act toward outsiders. . . . Let your conversation be always full of grace . . ." (Col. 4:5,6).

"Therefore, as God's chosen people, holy and dearly beloved, clothe yourselves with compassion, kindness, humility, gentleness and patience" (Col. 3:12).

When we lose our patience, we may also lose our opportunity to witness.

DREAD

MY HUSBAND WAS LATE COMING HOME FROM work last night, and I thought my insides would shake me to pieces before he came home. He's never late, unless he calls to tell me. After half an hour of pacing and looking out the window, I called his office, but the switchboard was closed.

Where could he be? I thought of the new girl I'd met the last time I'd gone to his office. She was younger than I, and had long, blond hair (bleached). She was almost disgracefully big busted, yet her face had the sweet innocence of a child. I'll *bet* she's innocent, I sneered to myself. I could see her now, sitting across from my husband in some secluded rendezvous, staring into his eyes. My heart pounded with jealousy. Hold on, my mind reasoned, you know he's never been a swinger. True, but if he's not with her, where is he? Forty-five minutes late!

I dialed his boss's home number. Nobody home.

Ah ha! I know! He's gone out with the boys. He used to do that — maybe he's going to start again. If that's where he's been, when he comes in, I told myself, I'm going to gather up the kids and go home to mother. I visualized myself and the kids, crammed into mother's guest room, with no daddy and no husband. Big, hot tears squirted down my cheeks. Surely he wouldn't do this to us. He loves us. Well, then, where is he? I went outside and looked up the street. My heart thudded as headlights came nearer and nearer, but with a roar the car went on by. One hour late!

The tuna casserole, shriveled and cold, looked as though it had already been eaten and rejected. Then, the thought I had tried to suppress surfaced. He had been in a wreck, of course. Dead, stretched out on the freeway. Tossed out of his careening car, he was now broken and bleeding in the dark. O my darling! Forgive all my cruel thoughts. I loved you so. More hot tears flowed. And then the headlights whitened our driveway. He was home!

I flung myself into his arms.

"Where have you been?!"

"I'm sorry, but the boss called a meeting just at closing time."

"Couldn't you have called?"

"He said he'd only keep us five minutes, and the other fellows didn't call their wives. But he kept talking, and talking — there was no way to get out."

So simple. So logical. So maddening! All that worry for nothing!

" . . . When the enemy shall come in like a flood, the Spirit of the LORD shall lift up a standard against him" (Isa. 59:19 KJV).

"Thou dost keep him in perfect peace, whose mind is stayed on thee, because he trusts in thee" (Isa. 26:3).

Satan, our enemy, laughs with scorn when we worry and forget to trust the Lord.

WHO AM I?

I THINK I MUST BE AN *EXTRA* ORDINARY person. People are always mistaking me for someone they know. It's giving me a multiplex complex. Last week, for instance, the phone rang.

"H'ya!" an intimate voice said. "How ya been?"

"Just fine!" I answered. I couldn't place the voice but I was sure it was a good friend. "How are you?"

"Just fine. I had a few minutes and thought I'd say howdy."

"Good," I answered. Who was it? Sombody at church? A neighbor?

"How's Bert?"

"Bert?" I asked stupidly.

"Your husband, silly!"

"My husband's name isn't Bert," I said, cooling off.

"Oh, come on, Rita!"

"I'm not Rita. You must have the wrong number."
Silence. Then,

"I'm sorry, but your voice — it sounds exactly like Rita."

Later, at the drugstore a woman yelled, "Hey!" and came running toward me.

"I can't believe how much weight you've lost!" She walked around me. I'm always trying to lose weight, but have gained two pounds this month.

"Why, you must have lost thirty pounds!"

"I think possibly you've got me confused with someone else," I said apologetically.

Her eyes narrowed and she looked at my face carefully. Then she began to blush.

"I beg your pardon! But you look exactly like my friend would have looked — "

" — if she had lost thirty pounds," I finished.

In the parking lot a man on the verge of hysteria loped over to me.

"Remember when I parked over there?" he yelled and pointed frantically to a brand-new station wagon with a big dent in one fender. His eyes begged for recognition and sympathy. I looked at the car I'd never seen before. "I haven't had that car for two hours and now some idiot has rammed it." A big sob shook him and I patted his shoulder. Since he thought he knew me I felt it was the least I could do.

When I got home our dog leaped up and wagged his tail. I'm glad he knows me. But then he doesn't rely on sight or sound — just smell.

"Are not two sparrows sold for a penny? Yet not one of them will fall . . . apart from the will of your Father. . . . the very hairs of your head are all numbered. So don't be afraid; you are worth more than many sparrows" (Matt. 10:29-31).

195

"O Lord, thou hast searched me and known me!" (Ps. 139:1).

Others may not know us — we may not even know ourselves! But God knows us intimately and individually.

THE OPEN DOOR

"DID YOU HEAR THAT THE PEOPLE NEXT door to me were robbed?" my neighbor asked as soon as she came in.

"No! What did they take?"

"Their TV, all their stereo equipment, cameras — just about everything they could pick up. And in broad daylight!"

"In the daytime!" I shuddered.

"Greg says I'm to keep the doors locked, even if I just come over here."

That afternoon when I went out to gather the eggs and feed the chickens, I locked the doors. After all, the pens are a long way from the house. It would be easy for a burglar to steal things while I was out there. When I came back to the house, I realized I had forgotten to pick up my keys. I put down the eggs and ran around to the front door and shook the knob. Locked, of course, and all the windows in front were shut and locked.

I went around in back and all those windows were locked too. It would be at least an hour and a half before my husband came home. Even when the kids came back from Good News Club, they wouldn't have a key. I looked over at my neighbor's house. She was gone, so I couldn't use her phone to call my husband.

Then I remembered the front bedroom window. I ran around to the side of the house, and sure enough, that small window was open. It was high and had a screen on it which opened from the inside. Well, I would just have to pry it off. I had to get in because now I could smell my stew cooking. Thank goodness the stepladder and a screwdriver were in the garage.

Just as I put one leg over the sill I saw a patrol car cruising toward me. I yanked my leg back out, slammed the window, and began to polish it with a Kleenex.

After the police car passed I looked around furtively, opened the window, and looked in our bedroom. It was at least a four-foot drop to the floor from the window edge. I put my head and shoulders through and hung there, wiggling and twisting, trying to get my bottom half through. When I finally scraped on through I landed hard on my arms and shoulders.

Outside, no one seemed to be watching. No wonder it was so easy to break and enter. Well, maybe not easy. I hurried out to the kitchen and checked the stew and then to the back door to get the eggs. Do you know what? I hadn't completely turned the little thing in the middle of the knob. All that commotion, and I hadn't even been locked out.

"[Jesus said], 'The thief comes only to steal and kill and destroy; I have come that they may have life, and have it to the full' " (John 10:10).

"Here I am! I stand at the door and knock. If anyone hears my voice and opens the door, I will go in and eat with him . . ." (Rev. 3:20).

Some of our friends are working hard to get to heaven. Let's tell them it *was* hard, but Jesus has already done the work.

CAN THE CANNING

I DREAD THE SUMMER. I DON'T MIND THE kids being out of school, or the heat, or the visiting relatives, but I hate the canning. When we first bought this half-acre, I was as enthusiastic as my would-be farmer husband. The plan was that he would plant and harvest, and I would can and preserve. The first year I scurried around like a bushy-tailed squirrel storing away goodies. At Christmas I gave everyone I knew some of my jams and jellies — but now they're all leery of my gifts.

"If it's jelly," they say firmly, "we still have some."

I don't blame them. I can hardly eat the stuff myself. None of it turned out right. There was one batch of plum jelly that looked just like Hawaiian Punch. In fact, I tried some with Seven-Up and it wasn't bad. I cooked the next batch longer, and what was left after it boiled over looked beautiful in the glasses. Clear and red, but I couldn't get a spoonful out. It had to be cut with a sharp knife, and when I finally got a lump of it out, it rolled around on my toast like a marble.

The peaches I canned tasted terrific, if you kept your eyes shut. They looked so terrible nobody would take any.

For some reason they turned sort of brown and huddled to the top of the jars like they were trying to get out. They looked so awful I was even ashamed to take them to church as white elephant gifts.

The tomatoes I canned were disappointing, too. In the first place my husband's tomatoes were odd. Some looked like faces in a horror movie and none of them ever got red. When he brought them in to me, they were all a pinkish-green.

"Shouldn't they ripen on the vine?" I asked.

"I have to bring them in before the bugs get them," he explained. "Put them in the window sill. They'll ripen." But they didn't. They tanned. My tomato paste looked like chicken gravy, and the pink globs in jars looked like something from a biology lab.

My husband is out in the garden now, hoeing and watering. It won't be long until he starts bringing in baskets of stuff for me to can. Wonder if I could get sick until canning season is over?

⸻

"Let us not become weary in doing good . . ." (Gal. 6:9).

"Whatever you do, work at it with all your heart, as working for the Lord, not for men. . . . It is the Lord Christ you are serving" (Col. 3:23,24).

No matter how distasteful our chores may be, if we remember we are doing them to please Jesus, we will do them heartily.

THE GREAT WASTER

LAST NIGHT WHEN I OPENED THE REFRIG-
erator and a can of chocolate syrup fell out, I knew it was
time to clean it. Cleaning the refrigerator is such a revolting
job. For weeks now, every time I've opened it I've gotten a
whiff of something. While trying to find a place to put what
was left of the chocolate syrup, I discovered what smelled
so bad: a little dab of sauerkraut and a shriveled-up hot
dog.

Resolutely, I took everything out, and it covered all the
counter space in my kitchen. As I looked at all the leftovers
and half-used jars of food, I felt disgusted with myself.
There was just no sense in having three open jars of
pickles, two bottles of catsup, five kinds of salad dressings,
a little dab of ironing, and a sack of tulip bulbs in the
refrigerator. And that was just the bottom shelf. I found
moldy lunch meat, moldy cottage cheese, and liquefied
jello, all tucked back under the meat compartment.

There was nothing in the meat compartment but a bowl
of gravy that looked like a piece of dried mud, and some
re-re-refried beans. There was a jar of jelly that had gone
back to sugar, next to the batteries. (A friend told me if I

wanted to make batteries last longer to keep them cold. I don't think it helps, because no matter what I want to use, the batteries are dead.)

When I opened the crisper, I'd never seen such an appalling sight. I couldn't stand to touch it, so I took it out and fed it to the chickens. I felt guilty letting all those vegetables spoil at today's prices, but the chickens enjoyed their meal.

I also felt guilty when I threw two coffee cans full of bacon grease in the trash, but the doctor said not to eat saturated fats. There was a piece of a cheese ball hidden behind an empty margarine carton. It must have been there since Christmas.

When I was all through cleaning, my refrigerator sparkled like a glacier in the sunlight. Of course, after I threw away all the leftovers, it was empty but hospital clean. Now I have to go to the supermarket. There's nothing to eat.

"He also that is slothful in his work is brother to him that is a great waster" (Prov. 18:9 KJV).

"There was a rich man whose manager was accused of wasting his possessions" (Luke 16:1).

It's a serious thing when we waste good food. But it's more serious, even frightening, when we waste the talents and gifts the Lord has given us.

PICNIC

IT WAS 100 DEGREES OUTSIDE, BUT IT WAS the last day we could have a picnic before school started. The kids wanted to go to a new park that had opened in our area.

"It's got a lake where you can go boat riding or swimming or fishing!" my son said.

"And playgrounds, too," my daughter added.

"I'm glad you kids like simple things," I said. "The best things in life are free."

Fortunately, I had a dollar they required for parking, but I had to say a firm *no* as we passed the boat concession, pony rides, fishing gear rentals, souvenirs, and soft drink stand.

"We've got Kool-Aid, remember?" I showed all my teeth. But my smile faded as I looked around at the park. It shimmered under the noonday sun. It would be lovely in a few years. There were shade trees all around, but they were only about four feet high and cast shadows two feet in diameter.

The park was full of sweating adults, crying children, and wet dogs, who shook themselves frequently. We found a table, and as I spread our lunch, I was glad I had remembered salt and mustard, but I wished I had remembered cups, plates, and napkins.

"How can we drink the Kool-Aid?" my daughter whined.

"We'll take turns drinking from the cap."

"I'm not drinking after any girl," son sulked.

"And I'm not drinking after you!" daughter retorted.

Thank goodness I settled that argument after I tasted the Kool-Aid and almost gagged. I must have added sugar twice.

"These samwiches are awful dry without anything to drink," my son complained.

"Here, eat this peach with it," I said.

"It has fuzz on it."

"Why don't you run over to that water faucet and wash it?"

"Mommy, can you do this?" my daughter asked. She was squeezing a ball of chewing gum (I didn't bring any gum) between her thumb and forefinger, then spreading them apart, forming long, sticky strands. I couldn't bear to look at her. Meanwhile, my son was stamping around in thick mud. He called,

"There's no water in this faucet! I can't wash the peach."

"Tough," I muttered. I shooed several heavy, determined flies off his sandwich.

After lunch we walked down to the lake to go swimming, but neither one of them would go in. I didn't blame them. There were floating cans, bits of paper, and many quacking ducks.

We walked a long way to the playground, but all the swings were taken. My son almost got into a fight on the slide, and my daughter stubbed her toe on a sprinkler.

I'm glad I took the kids on a picnic. And I'm also glad it's the last time they can go — for a while.

"But man is born to trouble as the sparks fly upward" (Job 5:7).

"About midnight Paul and Silas were praying and singing hymns to God . . ." (Acts 16:25).

Troubles are certain to come in our lives; but they are lessened if we make ourselves sing and praise the Lord.